Dedication

To Mr. Gurka, my biggest fan. I miss you dearly.
To my husband who has allowed me to feel
immensely without judgement and still looks at me
with compassion in his eyes. For my Cals thank you for
teaching mom it's ok to feel.

Preface

As I sit here looking up how to
write a preface many thoughts come to mind when
I read the words "be an open book". First umm corny,
second, what more could I possibly tell you about myself that
I haven't shared already? And last, you got this!

So, I did a thing and allowed myself to be vulnerable in a way
that literally scared the crap out of me. It was creative, deep,
and funny. I shocked myself and apparently my husband who
encouraged me to continue writing and create a book. Now I am
here reflecting and talking to you.

The idea of allowing began as an exercise from a book we were
reading in book club called "Yoga for the Wounded Heart". This
book is a beautiful display of vulnerability that pushed me to do
great things in my own personal journey with mental health. So,
the exercise asks you to create a conversation with an emotion
you are experiencing in the moment. You are instructed to ask it
why it is there, to acknowledge the difficult feeling and to let
it pass instead of ignoring (well what we think is ignoring) or
fighting it. In other words, being mindful. While I thought this
would have more of an effect on the members and that I would
facilitate and support, I was the one who benefitted most. While
writing I was allowing the most painful feelings to take space
and exit my body, something I had never allowed myself to do
before. The idea of acknowledging a flash back would paralyze
me, which meant that it was only right to block it. Except while
I was fighting it, the back corners of my mind and my body were
experiencing this trauma with great force.

I have PTSD from a childhood trauma that I won't go into but
will say that processing has been one daunting journey. Along
with PTSD comes a slew of emotions one has no clue what to do
with. It's like sink or swim or more clinical fight or flight. I have
learned through writing that each emotion has its place and is
ok to experience. Even the annoying ones like suicide, shame, or
anxiety. Being a therapist and generally empathetic person, I am
used to helping others with their battles and being encouraging
while internally struggling. Can you imagine everyday helping
people get over their trauma and ignoring your own? So, while I
hope this encourages you to take a first step in your own jour-
neys, this one was for me.

Brene Brown stated "Owning our story can be hard but not nearly as difficult as spending our lives running from it." Running is something I have become very skilled at. My flawed thinking was such: if I didn't say it out loud it didn't exist. I was raised to take care of my younger siblings and be an example so if I could make it, they could too. What would happen to them if I showed them I was holding in an immense amount of pain? I found that there was so much strength and support in my transparency than in pretending to be ok. The strength I found was authentic and appreciated. There are still days and weeks that I will run from a thought I truly do not wish to process or a feeling I cannot put into words. That's because I haven't worked out all the kinks and am very much still a human.

Last, how in the world did this become a comic book? I would say that I have a gift in laughing at the worst possible scenarios, or maybe a skill in making someone feel more comfortable about my pain? In life I have learned that your trauma can make people very uncomfortable, you can add humor so that it's not so hard to swallow or avoid it altogether. I wanted to feel immensely but I still couldn't stop laughing at the characters in my mind. During this process I would have the conversation but it wasn't dark and gloomy, it was real. This is who I am. I hope you have a better picture of me, but more importantly a clearer understanding of the ways in which people cope with trauma and mental illness.

TABLE OF CONTENTS

TRAITORS

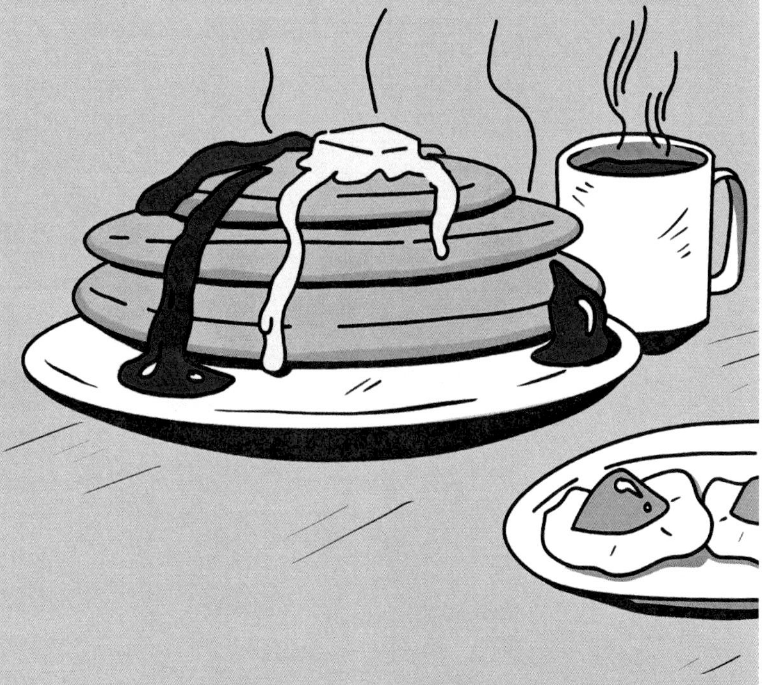

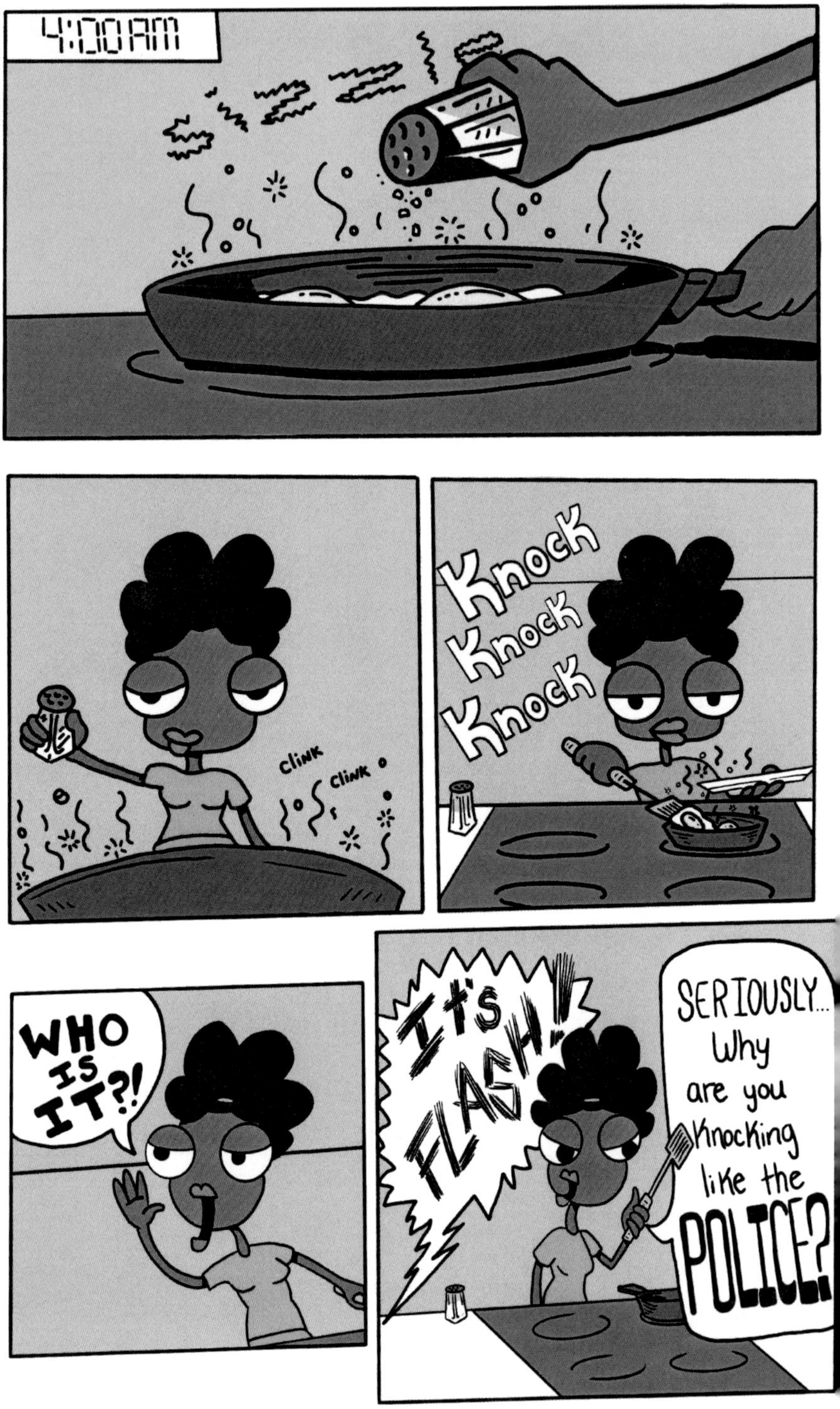
4:00 AM
CLINK
CLINK
Knock
Knock
Knock
WHO IS IT?!
It's FLASH!
SERIOUSLY... Why are you Knocking like the POLICE?

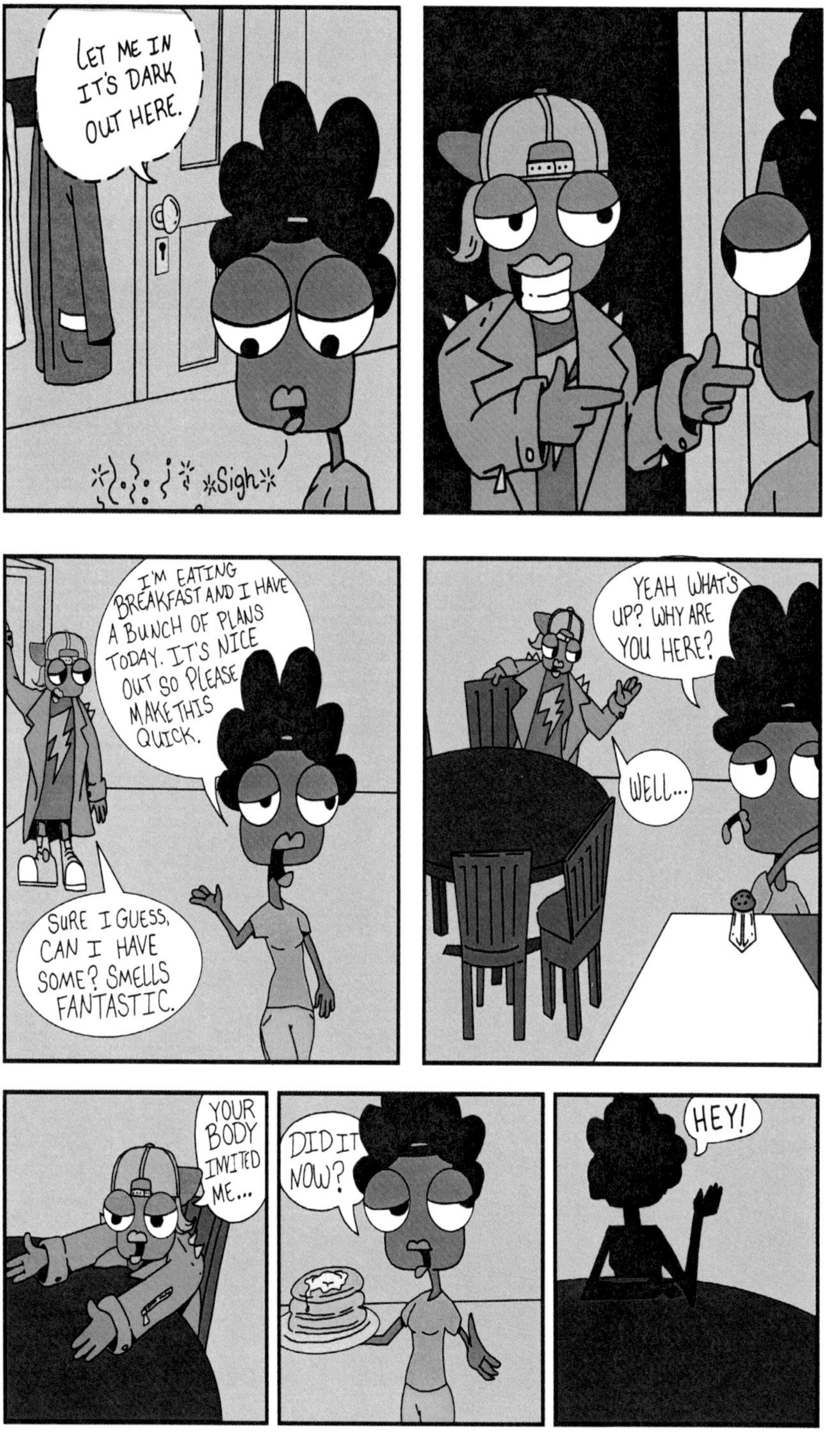
LET ME IN IT'S DARK OUT HERE.
Sigh
I'M EATING BREAKFAST AND I HAVE A BUNCH OF PLANS TODAY. IT'S NICE OUT SO PLEASE MAKE THIS QUICK.
SURE I GUESS, CAN I HAVE SOME? SMELLS FANTASTIC.
YEAH WHAT'S UP? WHY ARE YOU HERE?
WELL...
YOUR BODY INVITED ME...
DID IT NOW?
HEY!

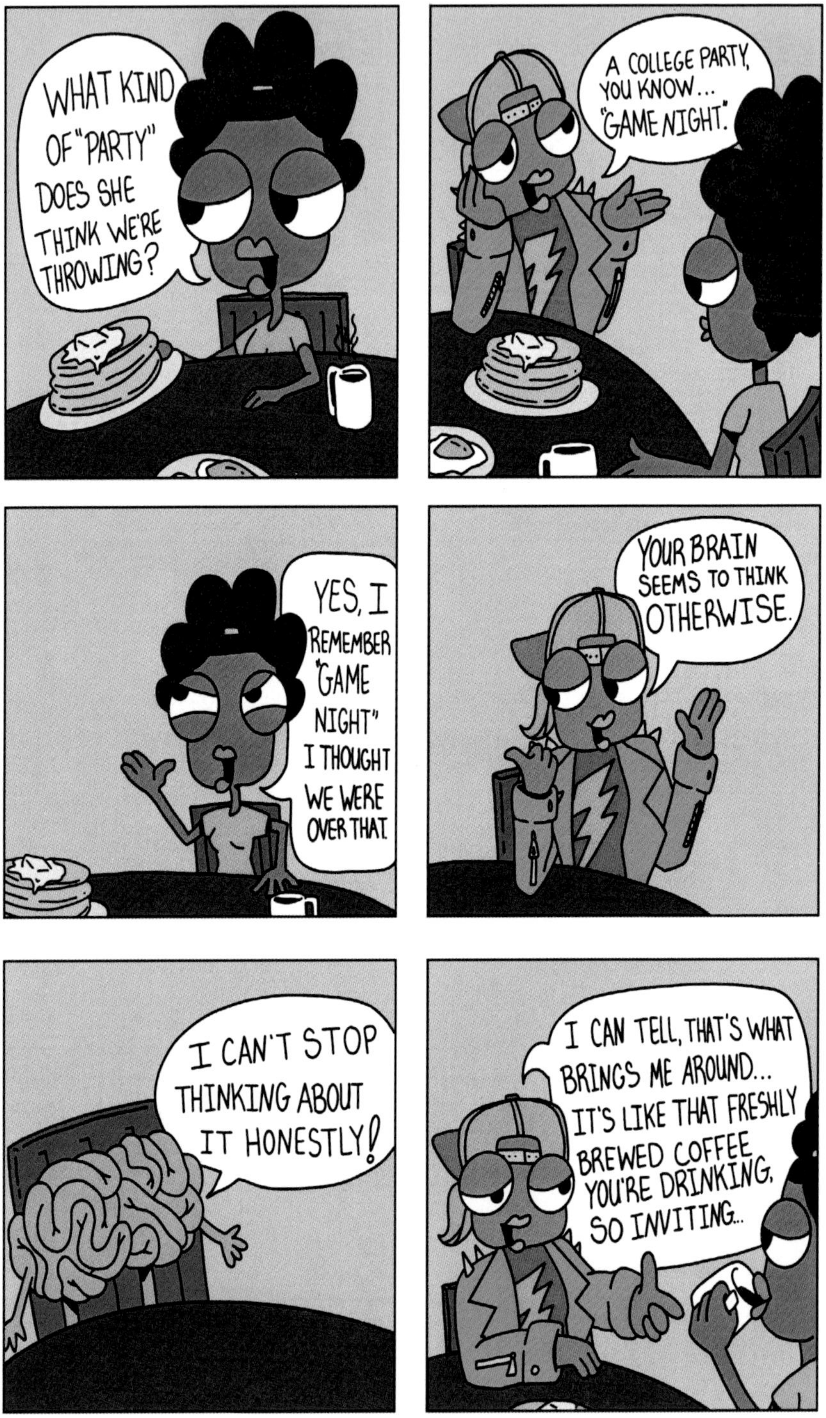

WHAT KIND OF "PARTY" DOES SHE THINK WE'RE THROWING?
A COLLEGE PARTY, YOU KNOW... "GAME NIGHT."
YES, I REMEMBER "GAME NIGHT" I THOUGHT WE WERE OVER THAT.
YOUR BRAIN SEEMS TO THINK OTHERWISE.
I CAN'T STOP THINKING ABOUT IT HONESTLY!
I CAN TELL, THAT'S WHAT BRINGS ME AROUND... IT'S LIKE THAT FRESHLY BREWED COFFEE YOU'RE DRINKING, SO INVITING...

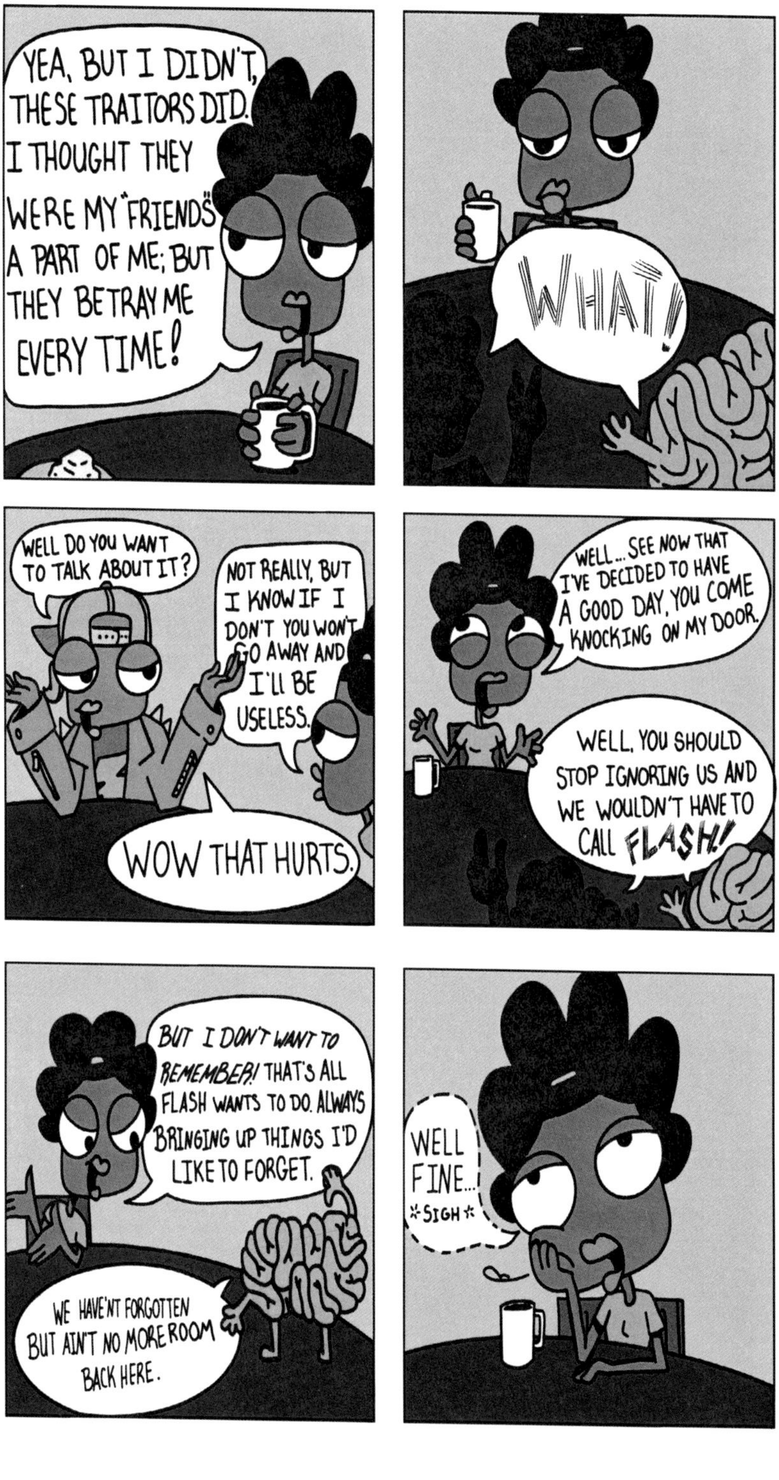
YEA, BUT I DIDN'T, THESE TRAITORS DID. I THOUGHT THEY WERE MY "FRIENDS" A PART OF ME; BUT THEY BETRAY ME EVERY TIME!
WHAT!
WELL DO YOU WANT TO TALK ABOUT IT?
NOT REALLY, BUT I KNOW IF I DON'T YOU WON'T GO AWAY AND I'LL BE USELESS.
WOW THAT HURTS.
WELL... SEE NOW THAT I'VE DECIDED TO HAVE A GOOD DAY, YOU COME KNOCKING ON MY DOOR.
WELL, YOU SHOULD STOP IGNORING US AND WE WOULDN'T HAVE TO CALL FLASH!
BUT I DON'T WANT TO REMEMBER! THAT'S ALL FLASH WANTS TO DO. ALWAYS BRINGING UP THINGS I'D LIKE TO FORGET.
WE HAVE'NT FORGOTTEN BUT AIN'T NO MORE ROOM BACK HERE.
WELL FINE...
SIGH

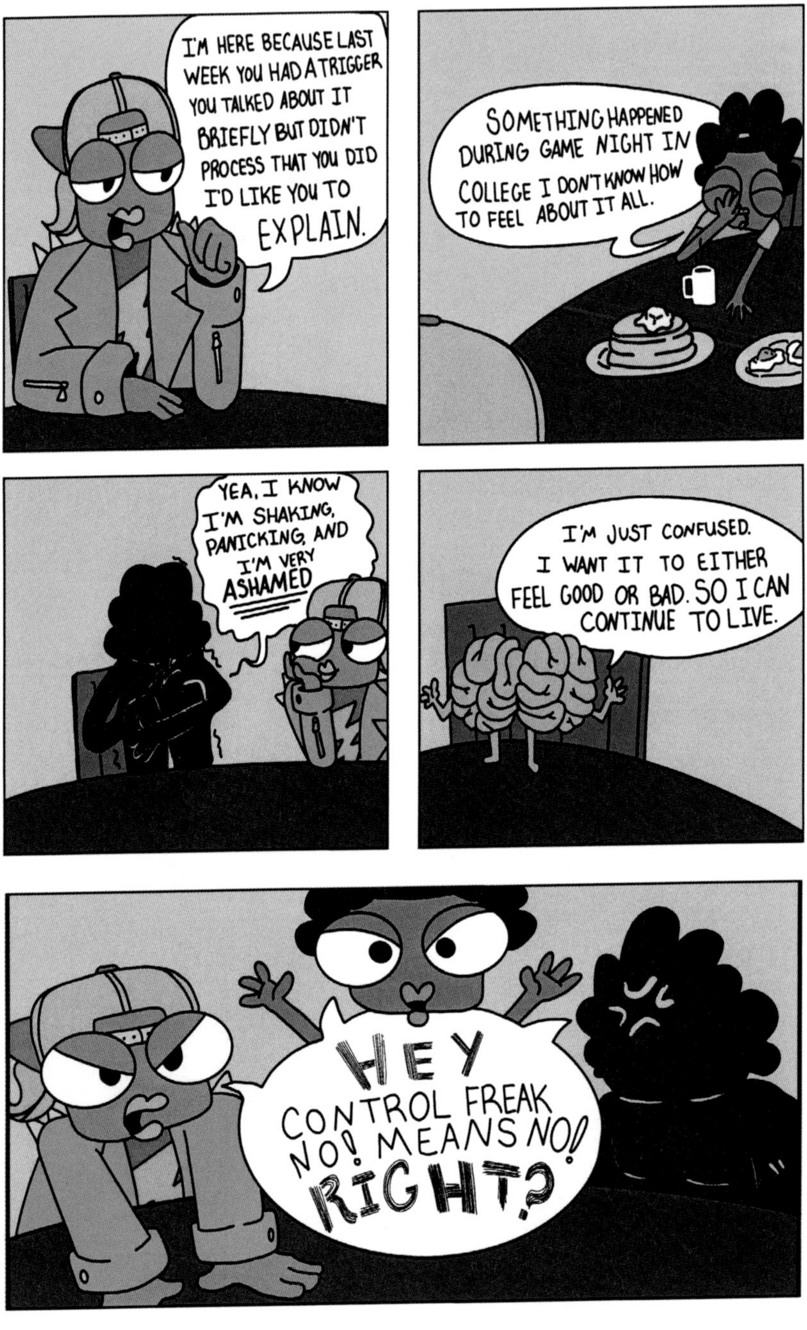
I'M HERE BECAUSE LAST WEEK YOU HAD A TRIGGER YOU TALKED ABOUT IT BRIEFLY BUT DIDN'T PROCESS THAT YOU DID I'D LIKE YOU TO EXPLAIN.
SOMETHING HAPPENED DURING GAME NIGHT IN COLLEGE I DON'T KNOW HOW TO FEEL ABOUT IT ALL.
YEA, I KNOW I'M SHAKING, PANICKING, AND I'M VERY ASHAMED
I'M JUST CONFUSED. I WANT IT TO EITHER FEEL GOOD OR BAD. SO I CAN CONTINUE TO LIVE.
HEY CONTROL FREAK NO! MEANS NO! RIGHT?

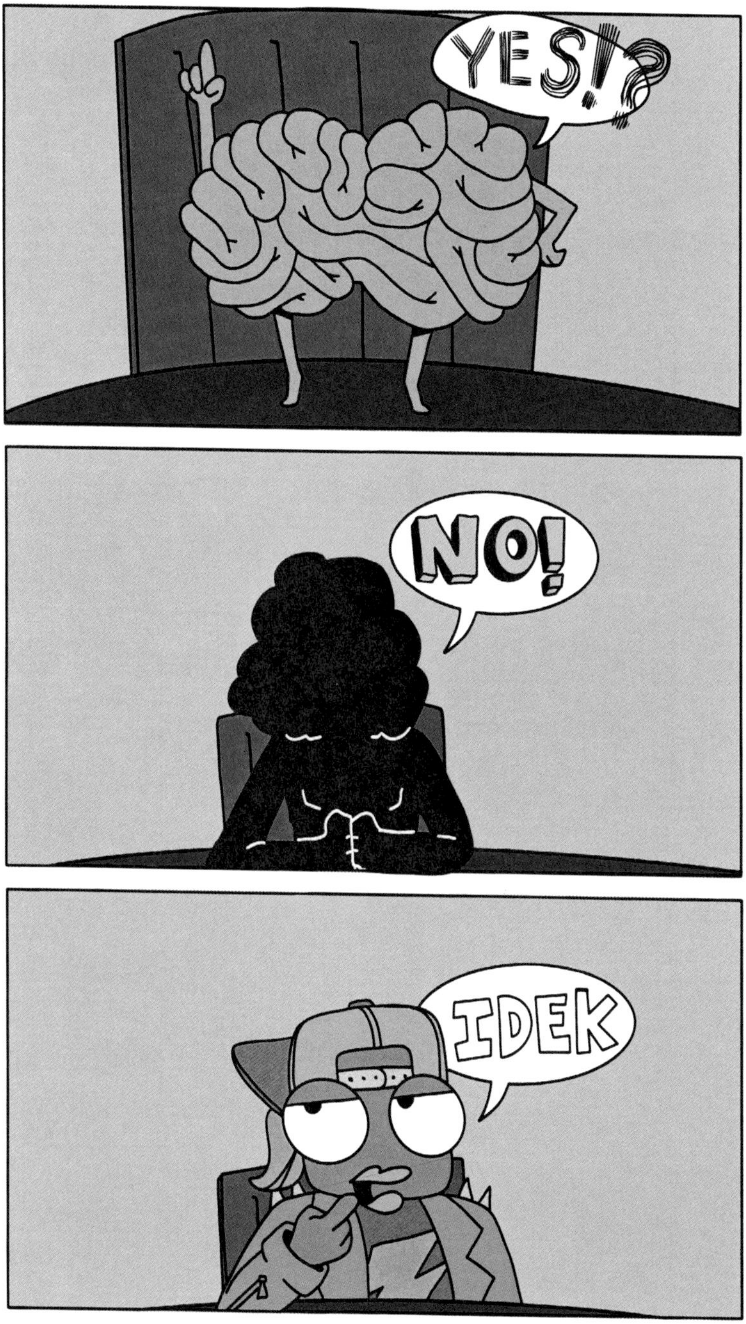
YES!?
NO!
IDEK

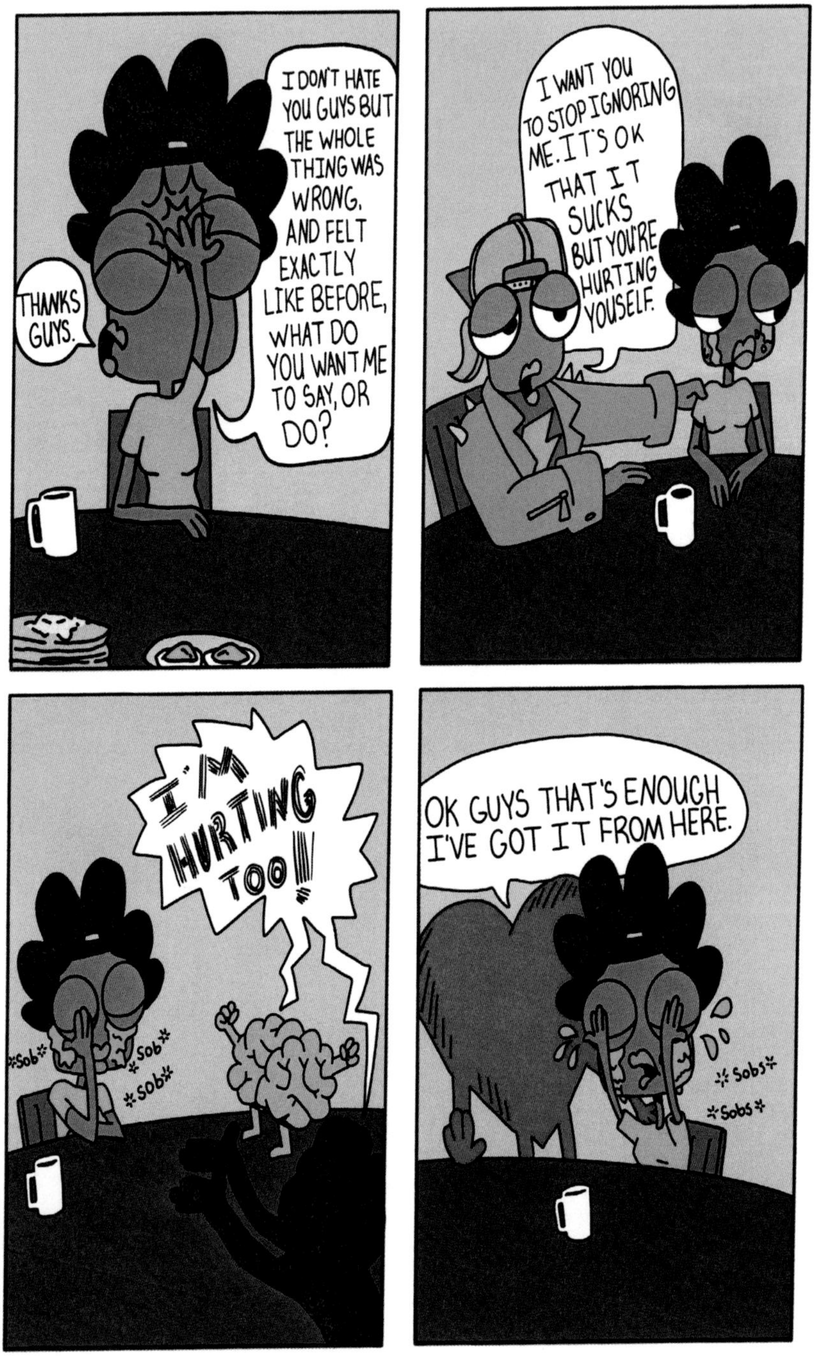
THANKS GUYS.
I DON'T HATE YOU GUYS BUT THE WHOLE THING WAS WRONG, AND FELT EXACTLY LIKE BEFORE, WHAT DO YOU WANT ME TO SAY, OR DO?
I WANT YOU TO STOP IGNORING ME. IT'S OK THAT IT SUCKS BUT YOU'RE HURTING YOUSELF.
I'M HURTING TOO!!
Sob
Sob
sob
OK GUYS THAT'S ENOUGH I'VE GOT IT FROM HERE.
Sobs
Sobs

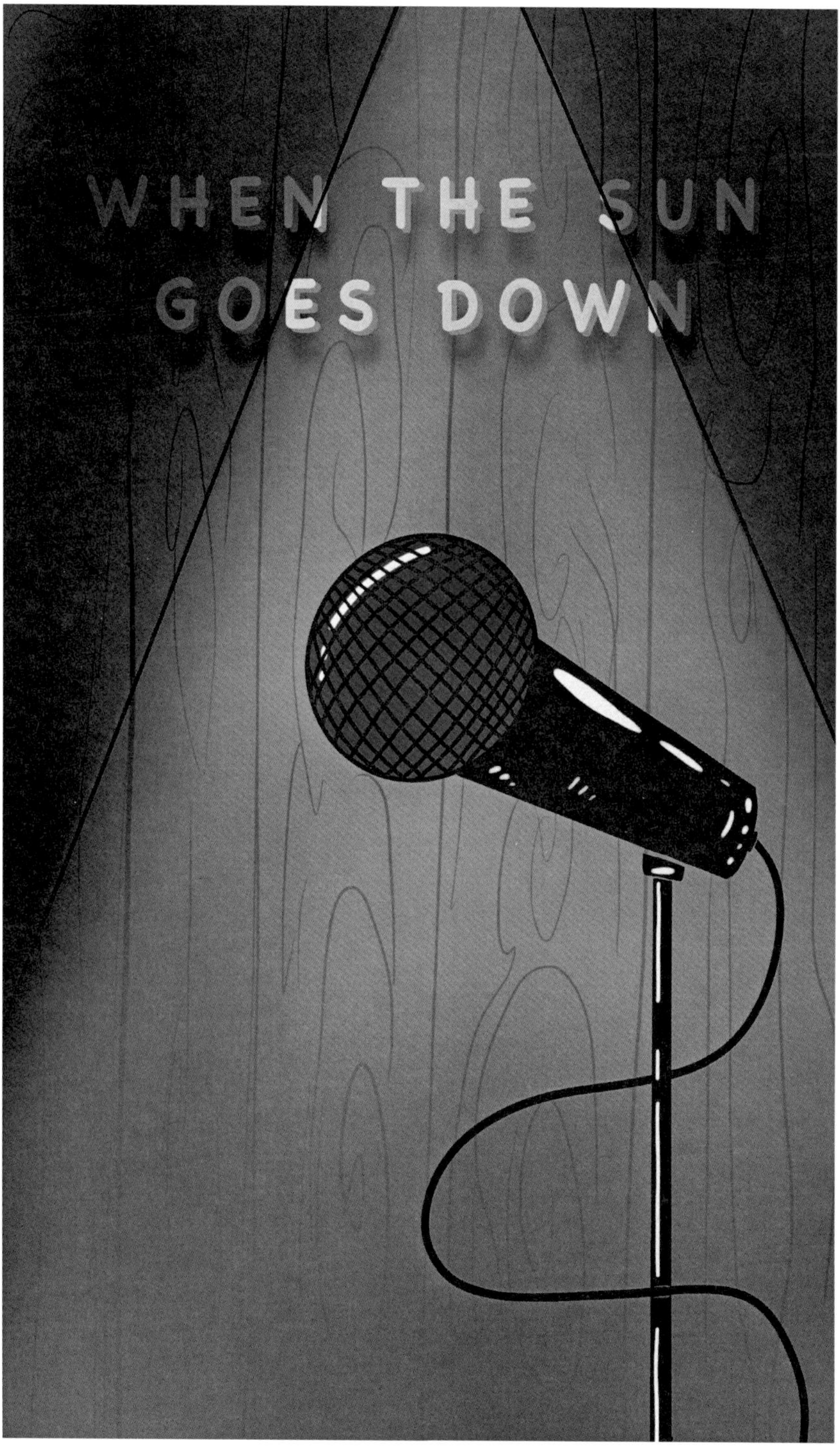
WHEN THE SUN
GOES DOWN

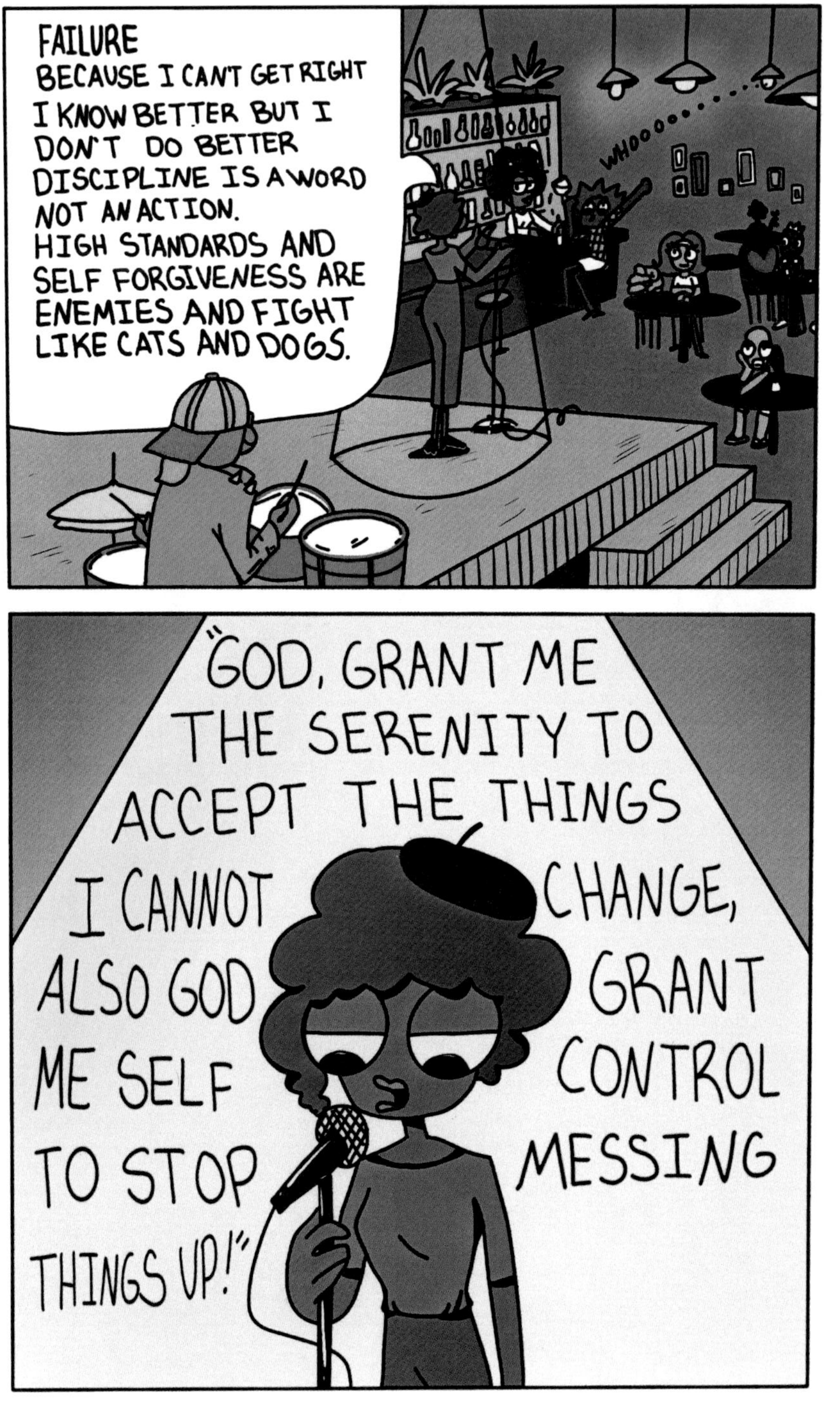
FAILURE
BECAUSE I CAN'T GET RIGHT
I KNOW BETTER BUT I DON'T DO BETTER
DISCIPLINE IS A WORD NOT AN ACTION.
HIGH STANDARDS AND SELF FORGIVENESS ARE ENEMIES AND FIGHT LIKE CATS AND DOGS.
WHOOOOO
"GOD, GRANT ME THE SERENITY TO ACCEPT THE THINGS I CANNOT CHANGE, ALSO GOD GRANT ME SELF CONTROL TO STOP MESSING THINGS UP!"

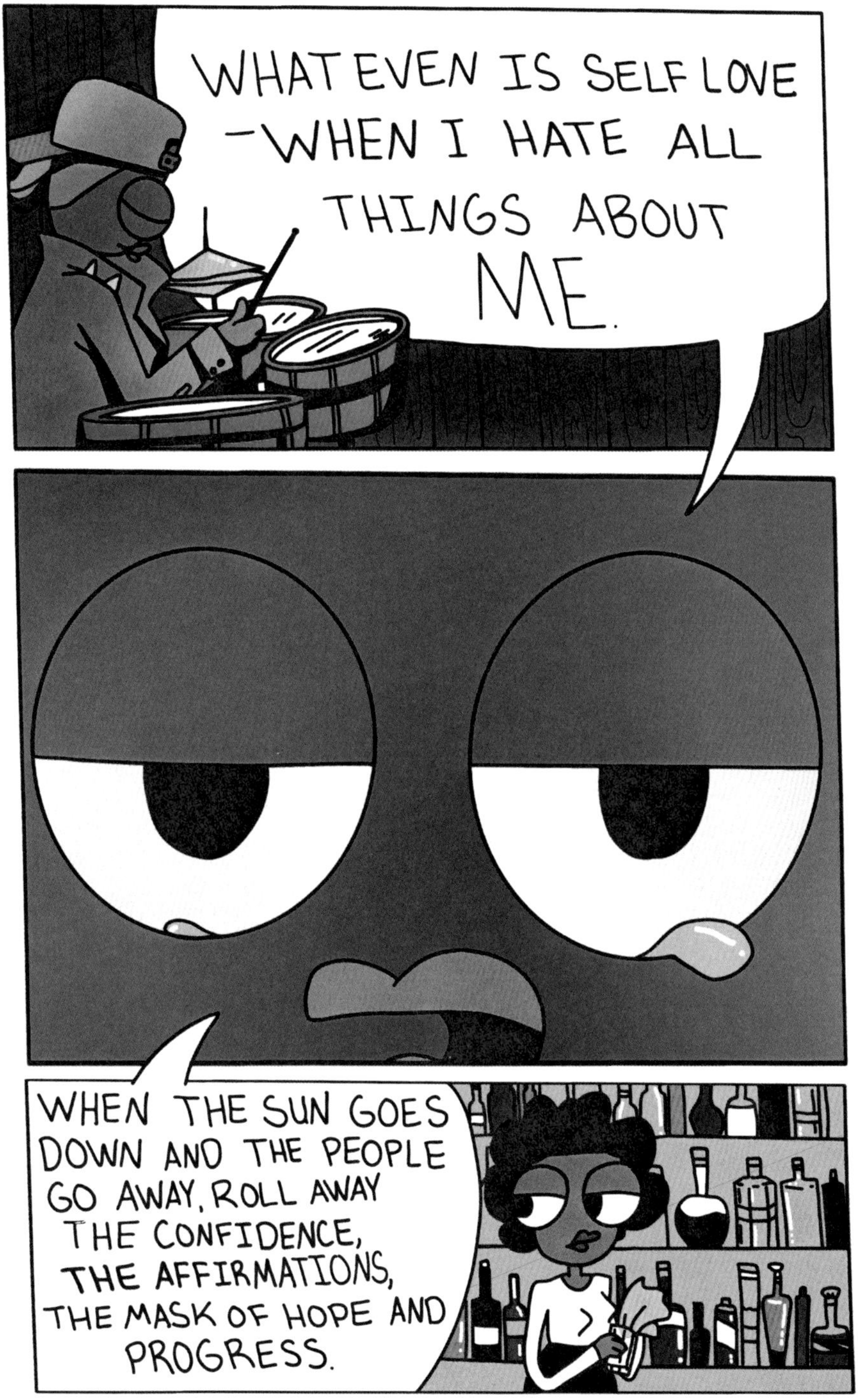
WHAT EVEN IS SELF LOVE -WHEN I HATE ALL THINGS ABOUT ME.
WHEN THE SUN GOES DOWN AND THE PEOPLE GO AWAY, ROLL AWAY THE CONFIDENCE, THE AFFIRMATIONS, THE MASK OF HOPE AND PROGRESS.

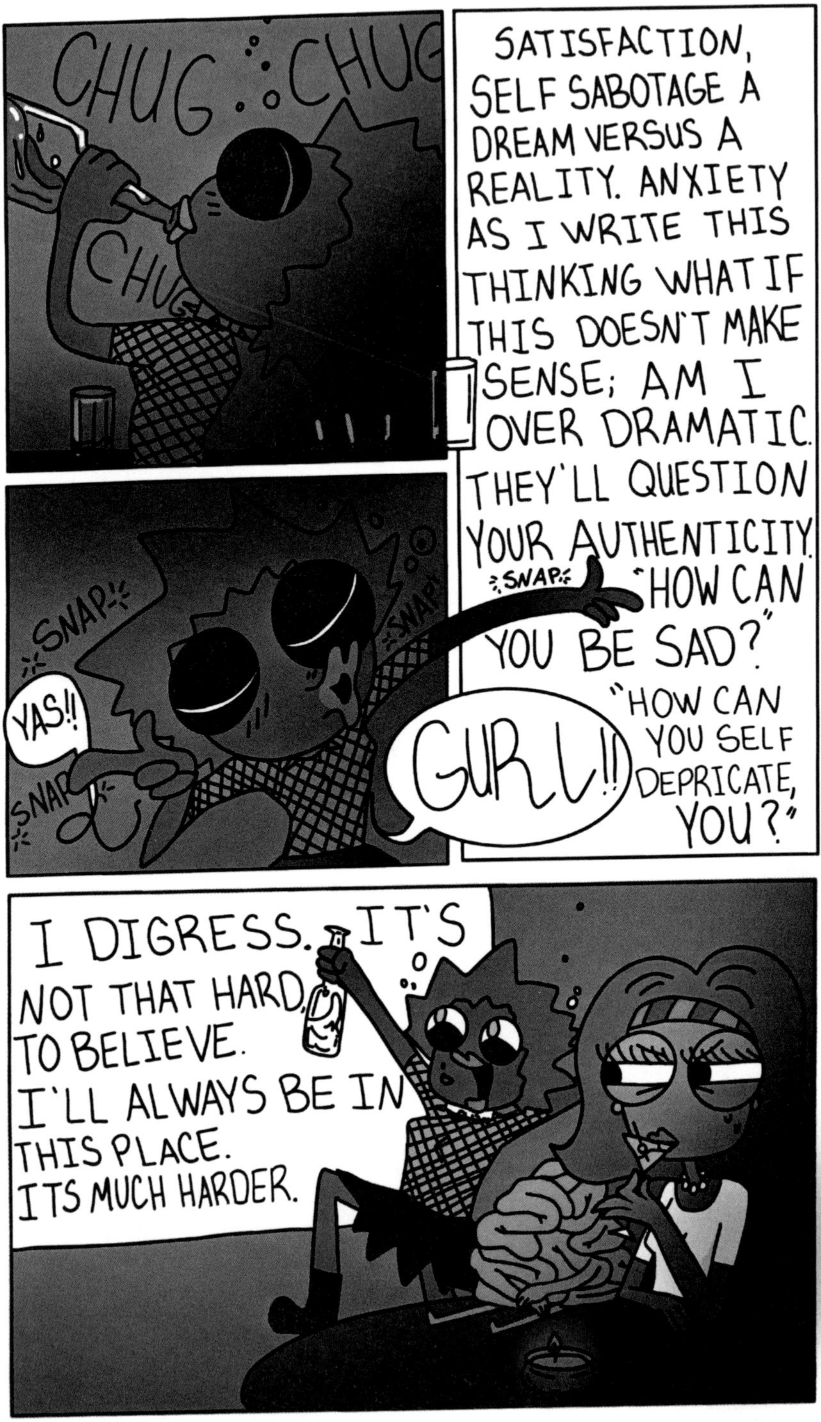
CHUG CHUG
CHUG
SATISFACTION, SELF SABOTAGE A DREAM VERSUS A REALITY. ANXIETY AS I WRITE THIS THINKING WHAT IF THIS DOESN'T MAKE SENSE; AM I OVER DRAMATIC. THEY'LL QUESTION YOUR AUTHENTICITY.
SNAP
"HOW CAN YOU BE SAD?"
"HOW CAN YOU SELF DEPRICATE, YOU?"
SNAP
SNAP
YAS!!
SNAP
GURLL!!
I DIGRESS. IT'S NOT THAT HARD, TO BELIEVE.
I'LL ALWAYS BE IN THIS PLACE.
ITS MUCH HARDER.

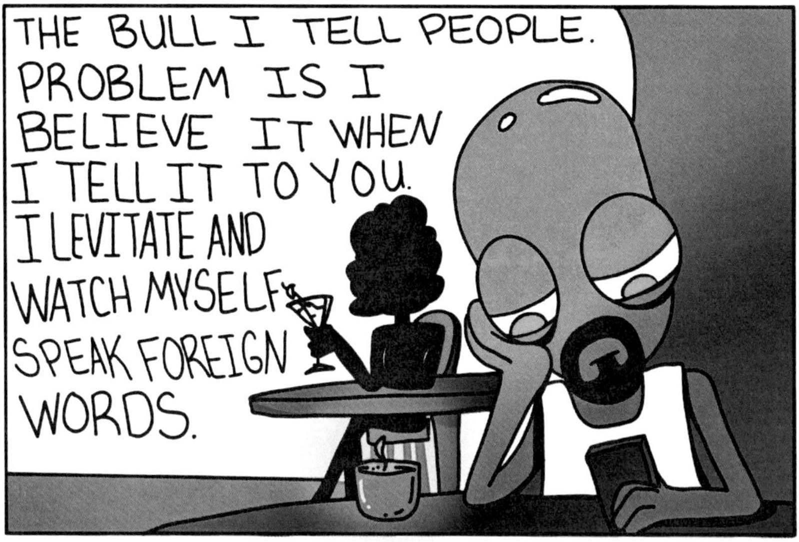
THE BULL I TELL PEOPLE. PROBLEM IS I BELIEVE IT WHEN I TELL IT TO YOU. I LEVITATE AND WATCH MYSELF SPEAK FOREIGN WORDS.

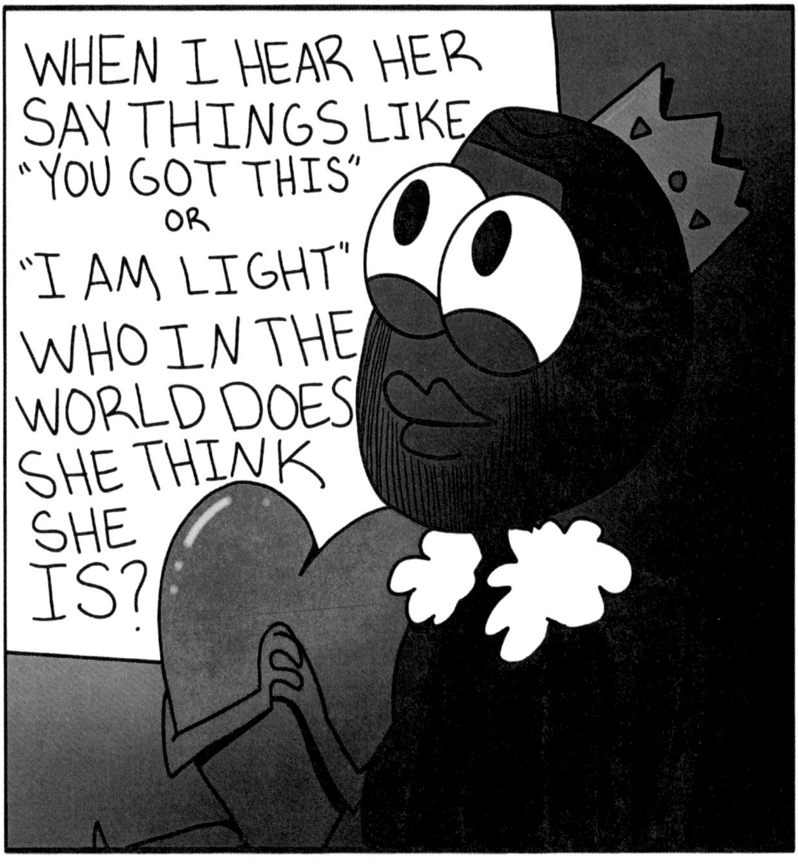
WHEN I HEAR HER SAY THINGS LIKE "YOU GOT THIS" OR "I AM LIGHT" WHO IN THE WORLD DOES SHE THINK SHE IS?

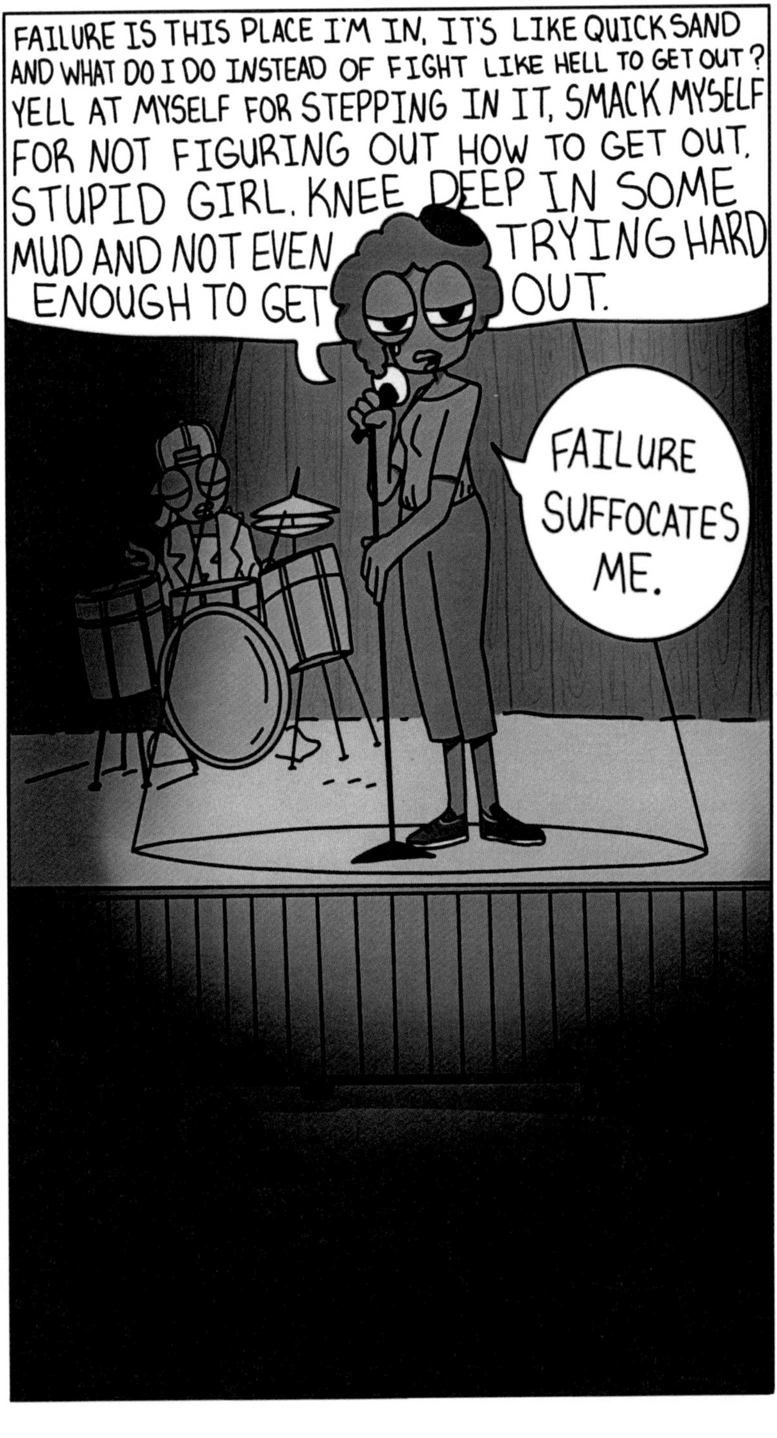
FAILURE IS THIS PLACE I'M IN, IT'S LIKE QUICKSAND AND WHAT DO I DO INSTEAD OF FIGHT LIKE HELL TO GET OUT? YELL AT MYSELF FOR STEPPING IN IT, SMACK MYSELF FOR NOT FIGURING OUT HOW TO GET OUT. STUPID GIRL. KNEE DEEP IN SOME MUD AND NOT EVEN TRYING HARD ENOUGH TO GET OUT.
FAILURE SUFFOCATES ME.

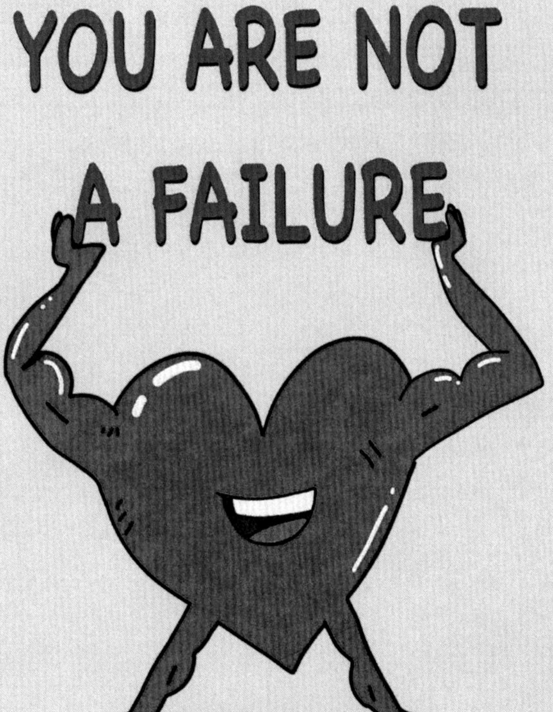
YOU ARE NOT
A FAILURE

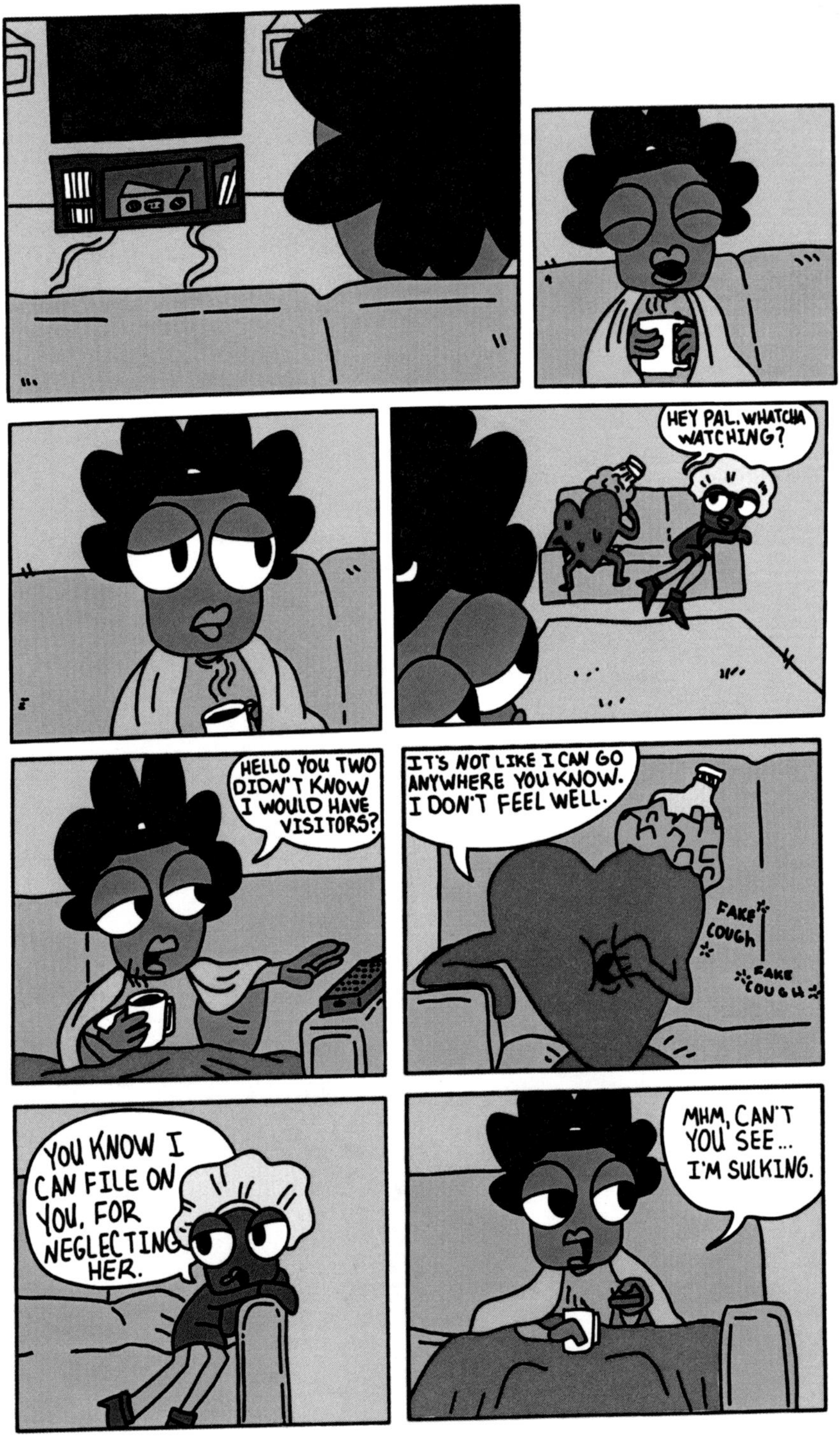
HEY PAL. WHATCHA WATCHING?
HELLO YOU TWO DIDN'T KNOW I WOULD HAVE VISITORS?
IT'S NOT LIKE I CAN GO ANYWHERE YOU KNOW. I DON'T FEEL WELL.
FAKE COUGH
FAKE COUGH
YOU KNOW I CAN FILE ON YOU, FOR NEGLECTING HER.
MHM, CAN'T YOU SEE... I'M SULKING.

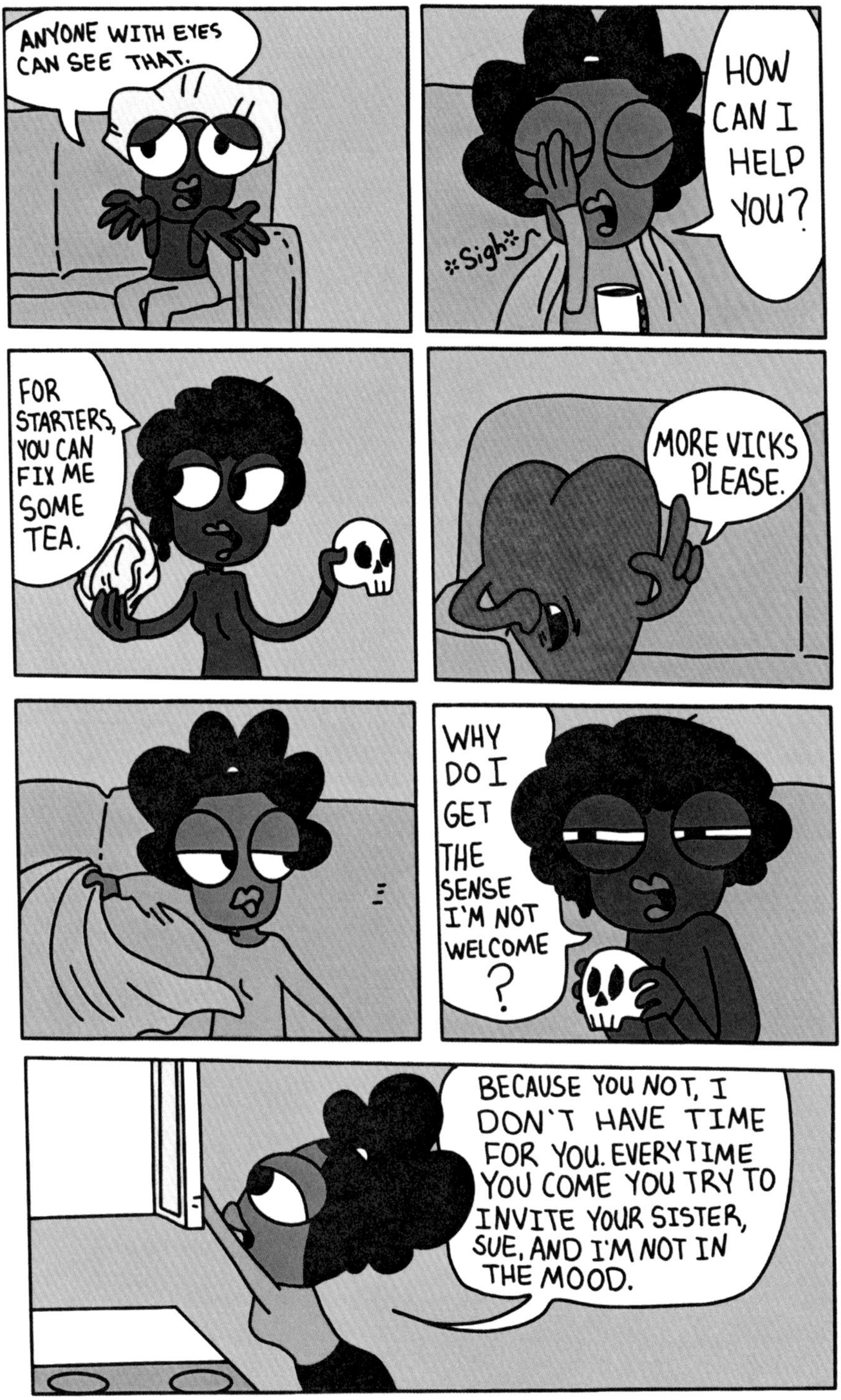
ANYONE WITH EYES CAN SEE THAT.
HOW CAN I HELP YOU?
Sigh
FOR STARTERS, YOU CAN FIX ME SOME TEA.
MORE VICKS PLEASE.
WHY DO I GET THE SENSE I'M NOT WELCOME?
BECAUSE YOU NOT, I DON'T HAVE TIME FOR YOU. EVERYTIME YOU COME YOU TRY TO INVITE YOUR SISTER, SUE, AND I'M NOT IN THE MOOD.

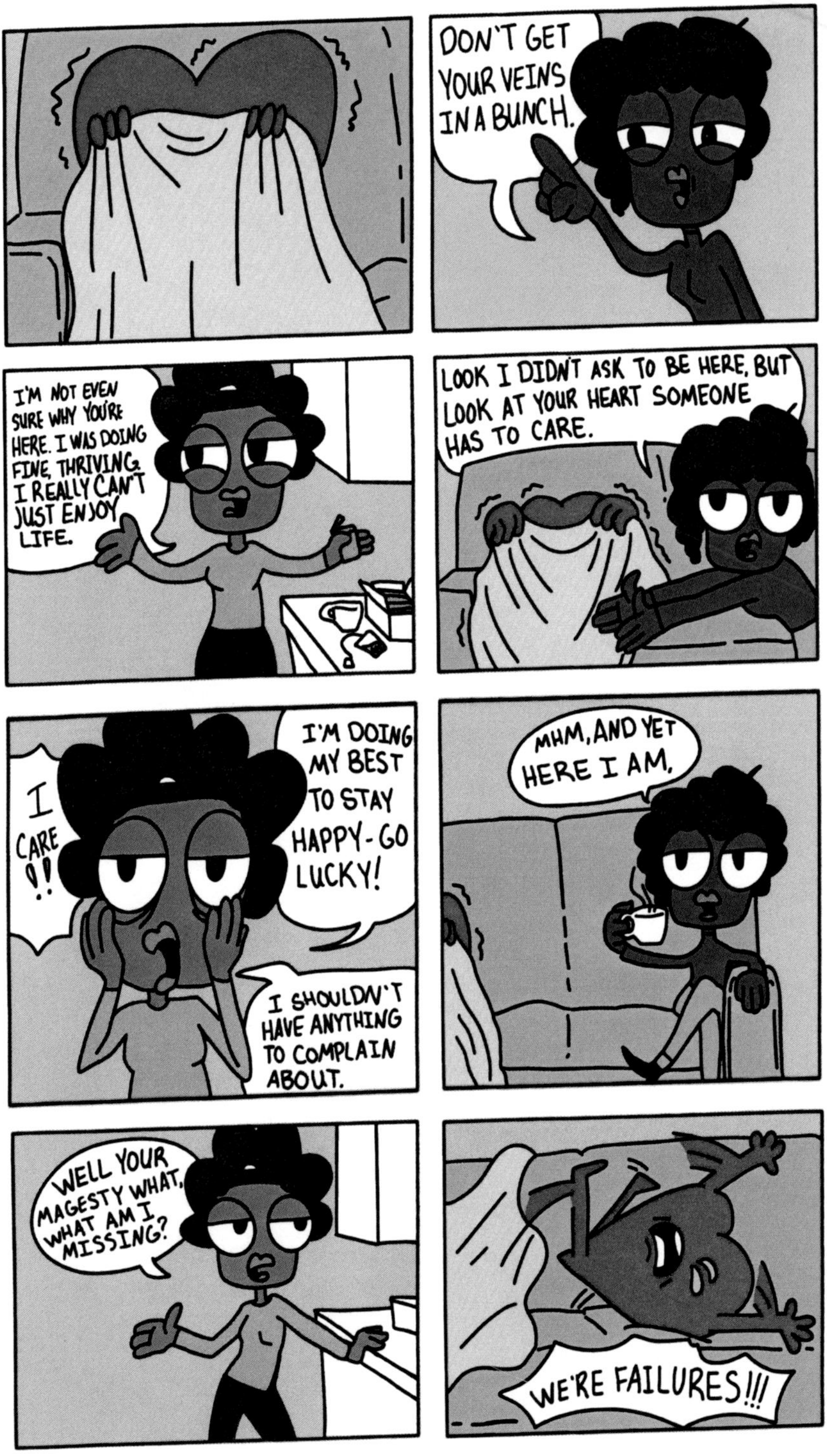
DON'T GET YOUR VEINS IN A BUNCH.
I'M NOT EVEN SURE WHY YOU'RE HERE. I WAS DOING FINE, THRIVING. I REALLY CAN'T JUST ENJOY LIFE.
LOOK I DIDN'T ASK TO BE HERE, BUT LOOK AT YOUR HEART SOMEONE HAS TO CARE.
I CARE!!
I'M DOING MY BEST TO STAY HAPPY-GO LUCKY!
I SHOULDN'T HAVE ANYTHING TO COMPLAIN ABOUT.
MHM, AND YET HERE I AM,
WELL YOUR MAGESTY WHAT, WHAT AM I MISSING?
WE'RE FAILURES!!!

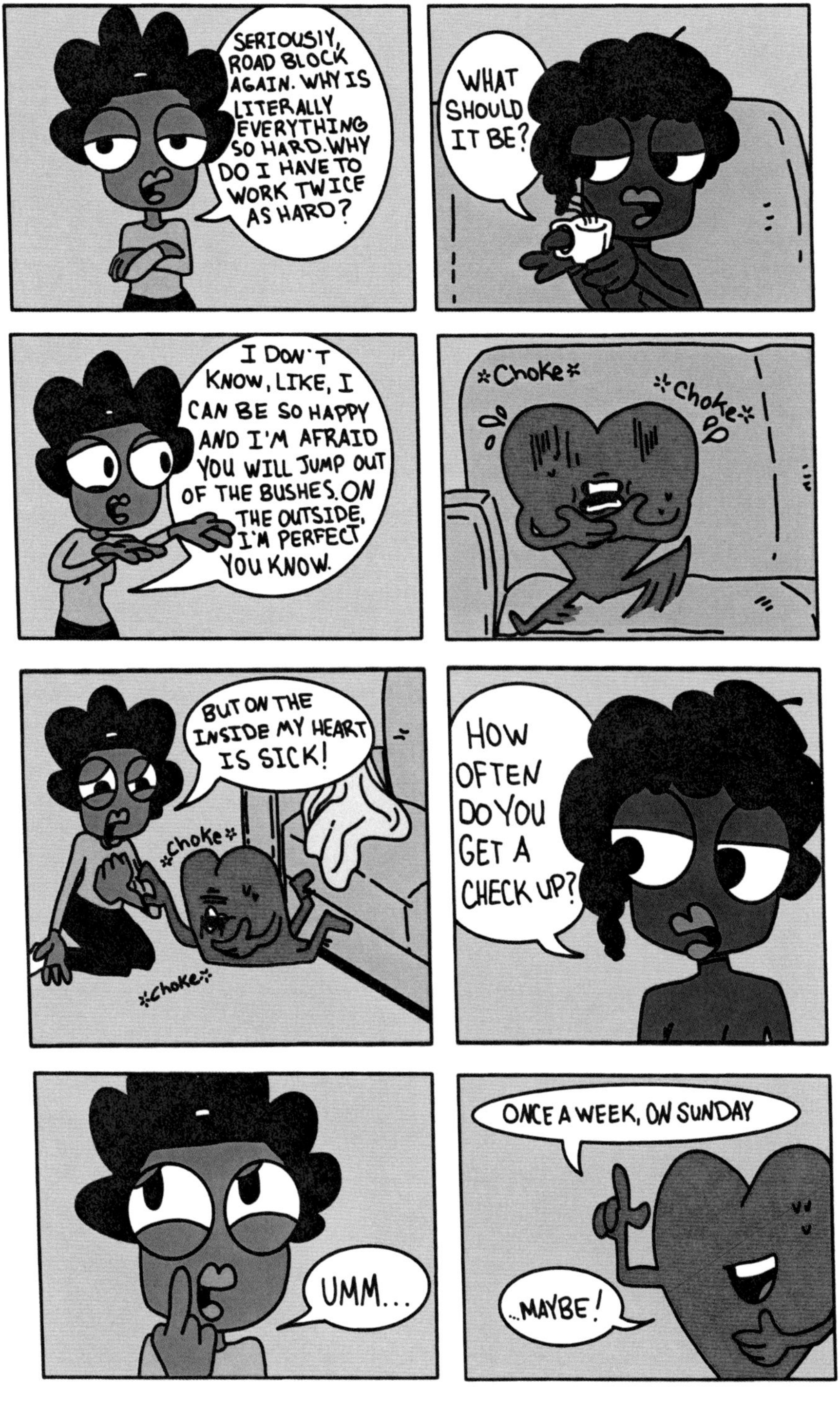
SERIOUSlY, ROAD BLOCK AGAIN. WHY IS LITERALLY EVERYTHING SO HARD. WHY DO I HAVE TO WORK TWICE AS HARD?
WHAT SHOULD IT BE?
I DON'T KNOW, LIKE, I CAN BE SO HAPPY AND I'M AFRAID YOU WILL JUMP OUT OF THE BUSHES. ON THE OUTSIDE, I'M PERFECT YOU KNOW.
Choke
Choke
BUT ON THE INSIDE MY HEART IS SICK!
Choke
Choke
HOW OFTEN DO YOU GET A CHECK UP?
UMM...
ONCE A WEEK, ON SUNDAY
...MAYBE!

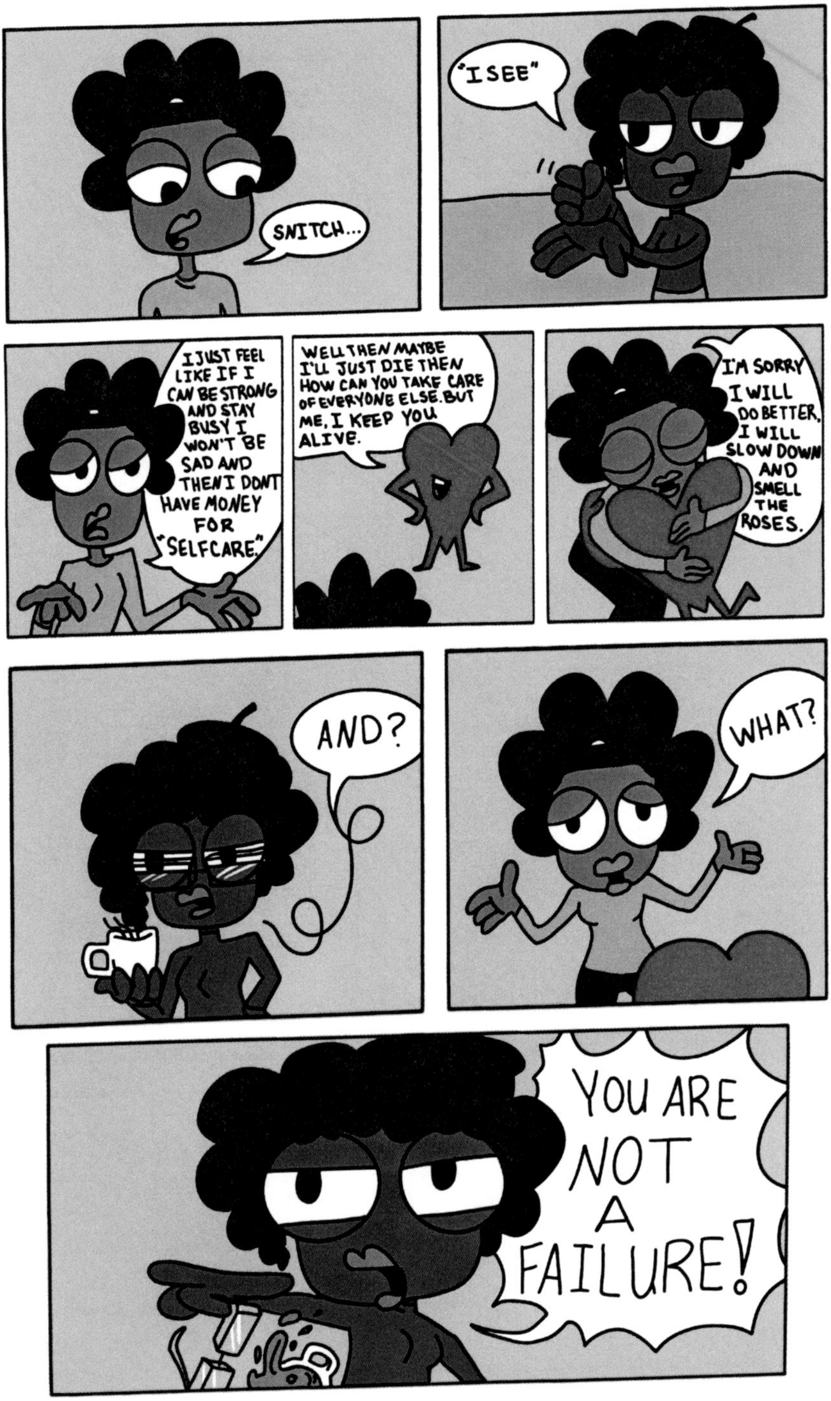
SNITCH...
"I SEE"
I JUST FEEL LIKE IF I CAN BE STRONG AND STAY BUSY I WON'T BE SAD AND THEN I DONT HAVE MONEY FOR "SELFCARE."
WELL THEN MAYBE I'LL JUST DIE THEN HOW CAN YOU TAKE CARE OF EVERYONE ELSE. BUT ME, I KEEP YOU ALIVE.
I'M SORRY I WILL DO BETTER, I WILL SLOW DOWN AND SMELL THE ROSES.
AND?
WHAT?
YOU ARE NOT A FAILURE!

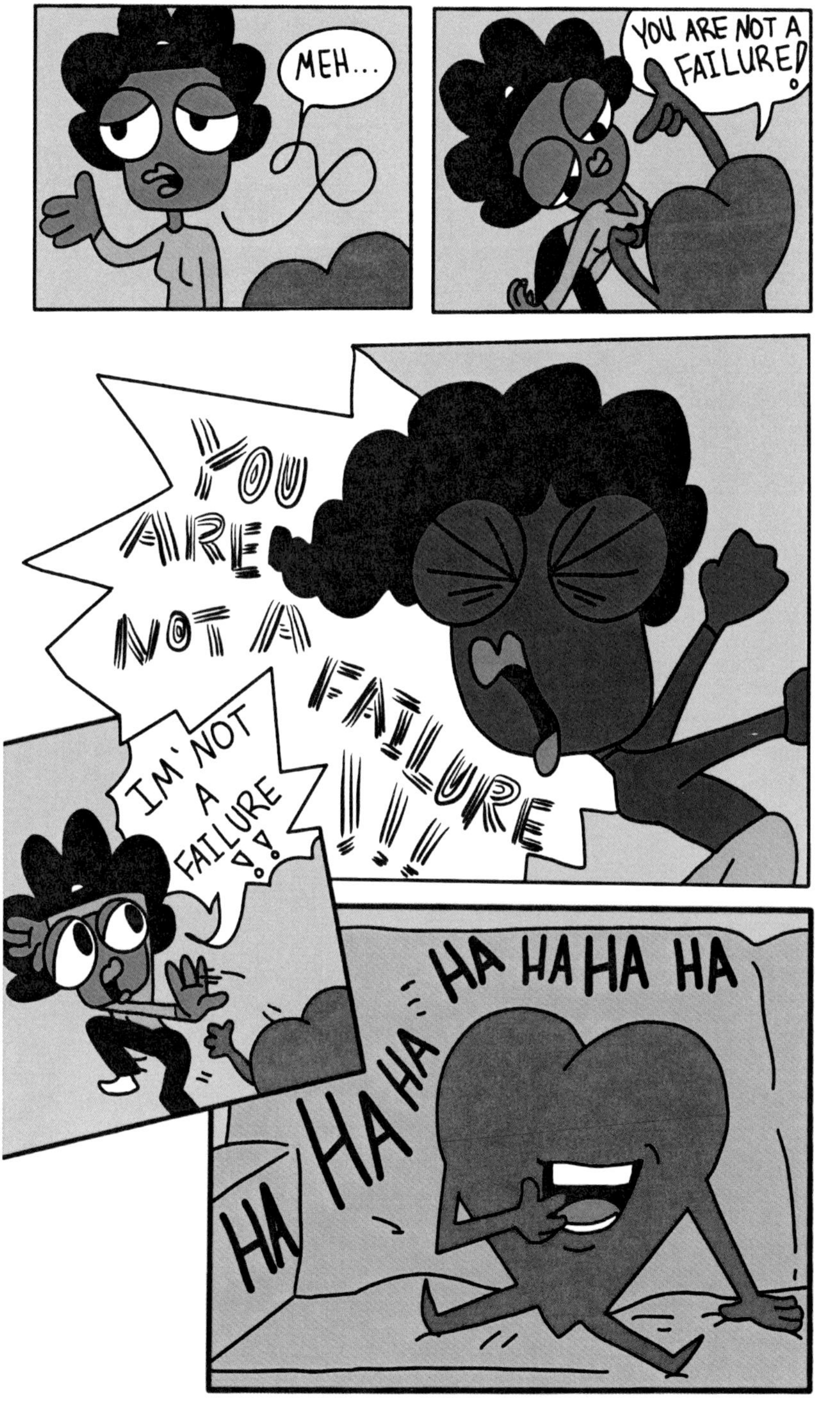
MEH...
YOU ARE NOT A FAILURE!
YOU ARE NOT A FAILURE!!!
I'M NOT A FAILURE!!
HA HA HA HA
HA HA HA HA

THE PROMISE
KEEPER

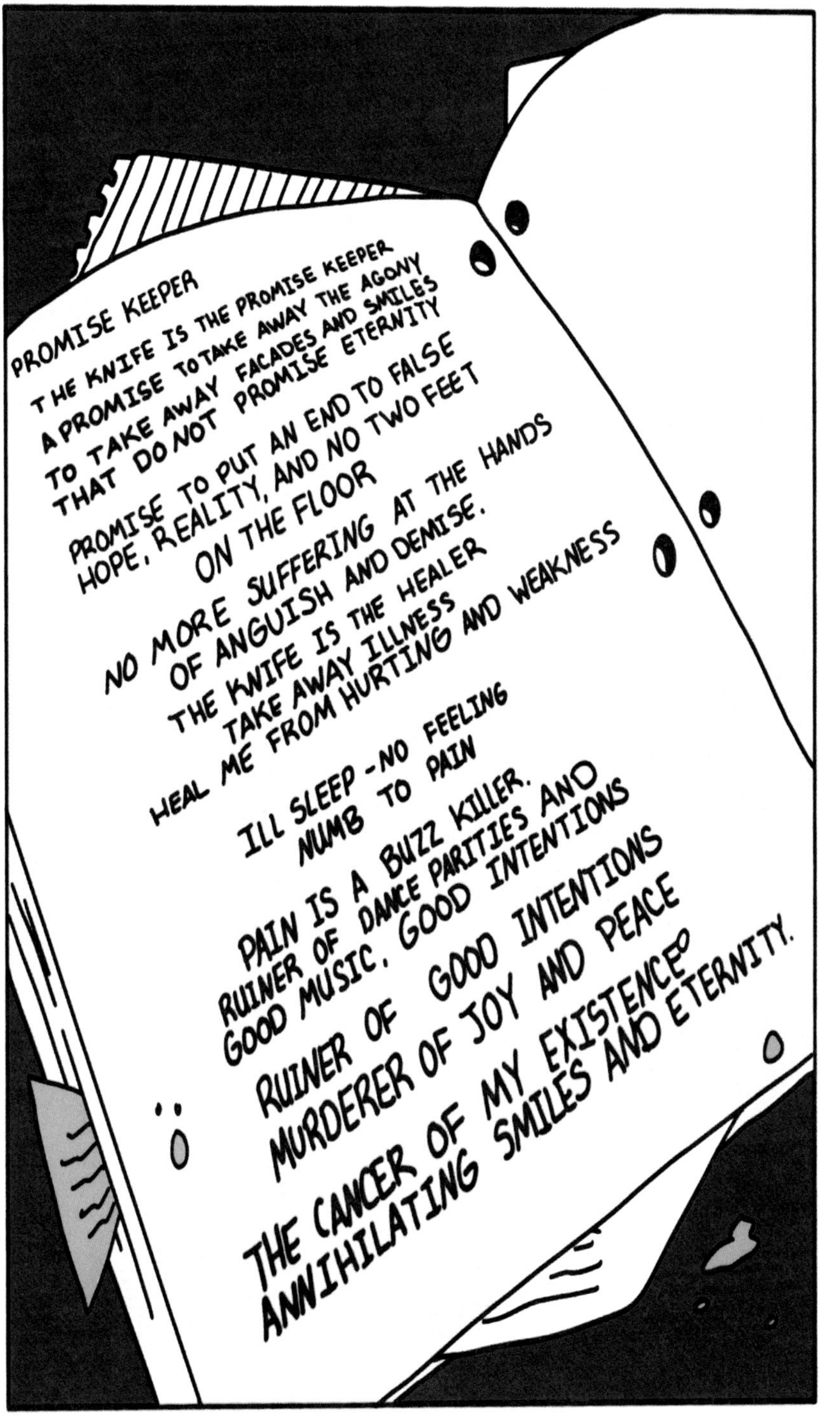
PROMISE KEEPER
THE KNIFE IS THE PROMISE KEEPER
A PROMISE TO TAKE AWAY THE AGONY
TO TAKE AWAY FACADES AND SMILES
THAT DO NOT PROMISE ETERNITY
PROMISE TO PUT AN END TO FALSE
HOPE, REALITY, AND NO TWO FEET
ON THE FLOOR
NO MORE SUFFERING AT THE HANDS
OF ANGUISH AND DEMISE.
THE KNIFE IS THE HEALER
TAKE AWAY ILLNESS
HEAL ME FROM HURTING AND WEAKNESS
ILL SLEEP - NO FEELING
NUMB TO PAIN
PAIN IS A BUZZ KILLER.
RUINER OF DANCE PARITIES AND
GOOD MUSIC. GOOD INTENTIONS
RUINER OF GOOD INTENTIONS
MURDERER OF JOY AND PEACE
THE CANCER OF MY EXISTENCE
ANNIHILATING SMILES AND ETERNITY.

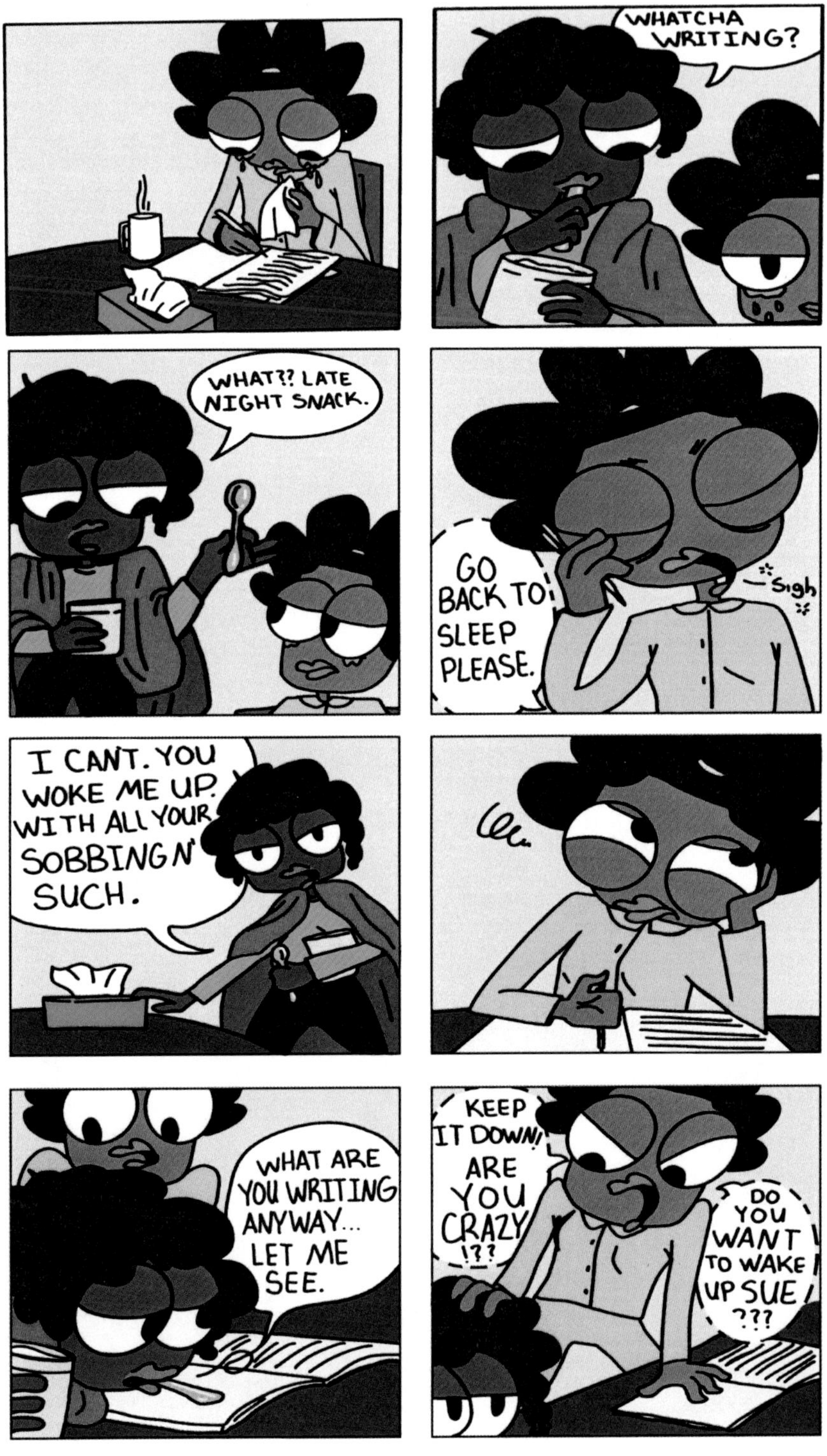
WHATCHA WRITING?
WHAT?? LATE NIGHT SNACK.
GO BACK TO SLEEP PLEASE.
Sigh
I CAN'T. YOU WOKE ME UP. WITH ALL YOUR SOBBING N' SUCH.
WHAT ARE YOU WRITING ANYWAY... LET ME SEE.
KEEP IT DOWN! ARE YOU CRAZY !??
DO YOU WANT TO WAKE UP SUE ???

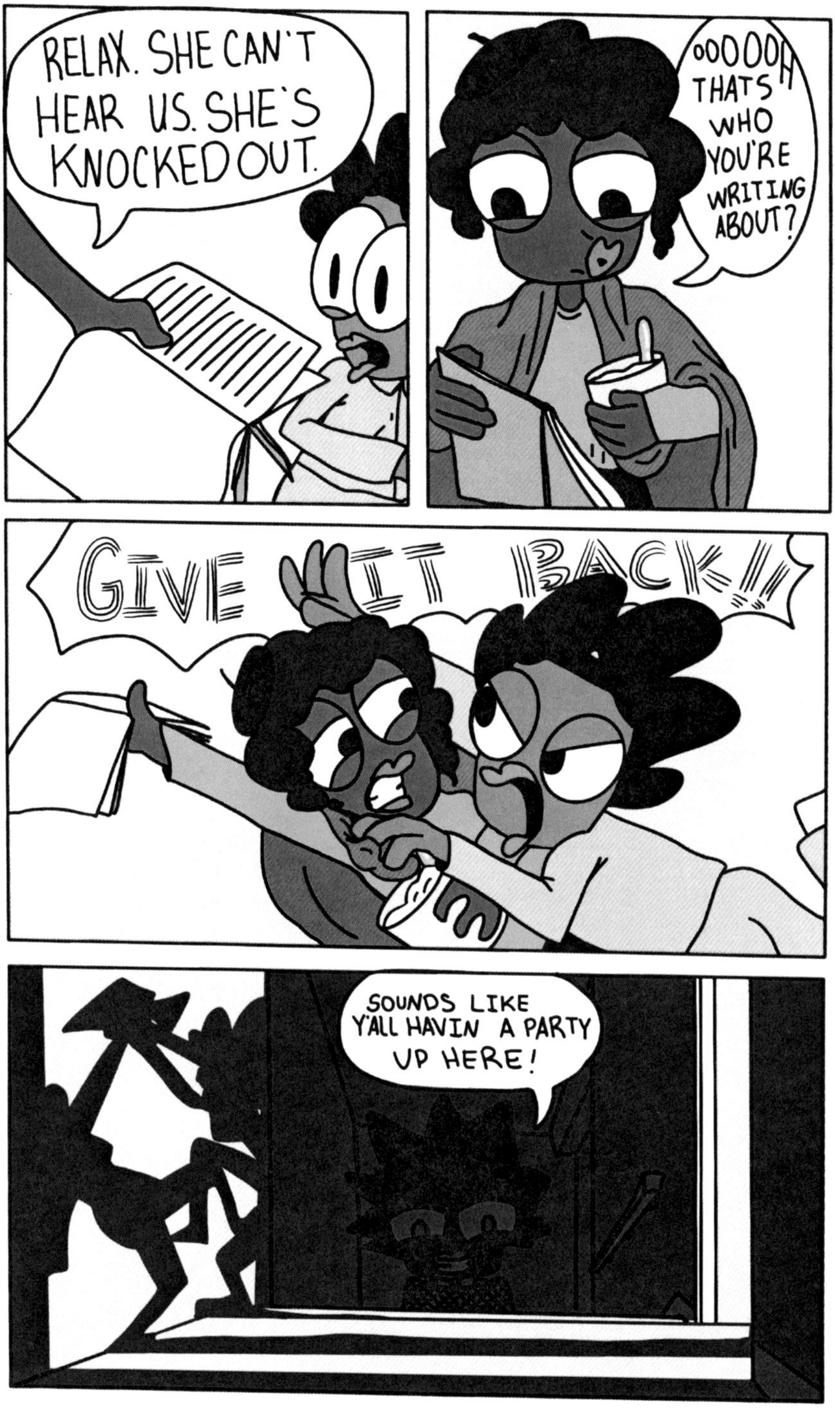
RELAX. SHE CAN'T HEAR US. SHE'S KNOCKED OUT.
OOOOOH THATS WHO YOU'RE WRITING ABOUT?
GIVE IT BACK!!
SOUNDS LIKE Y'ALL HAVIN A PARTY UP HERE!

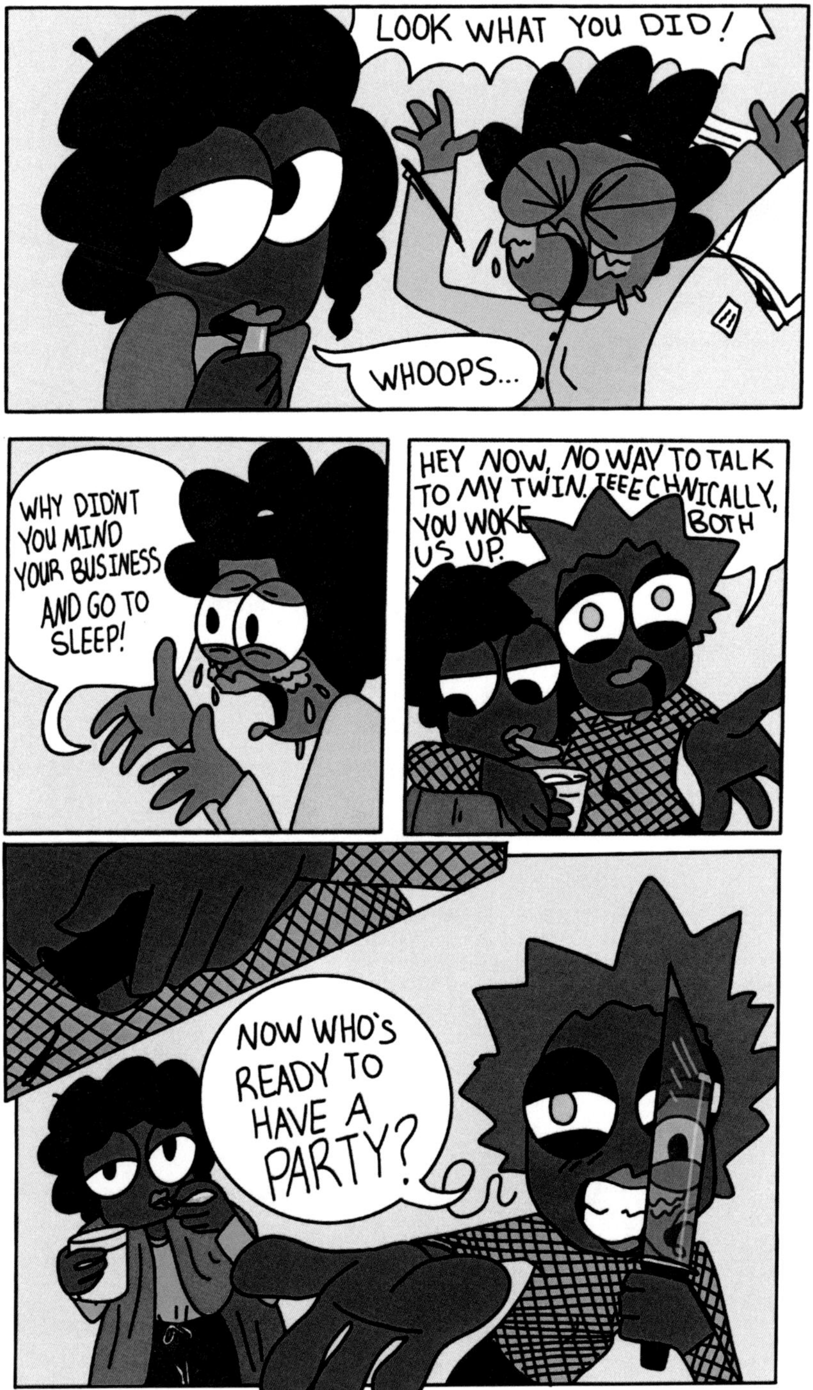
LOOK WHAT YOU DID!
WHOOPS...
WHY DIDN'T YOU MIND YOUR BUSINESS AND GO TO SLEEP!
HEY NOW, NO WAY TO TALK TO MY TWIN. TEEECHNICALLY, YOU WOKE BOTH US UP.
NOW WHO'S READY TO HAVE A PARTY?

OVERWHELMING ANXIETY

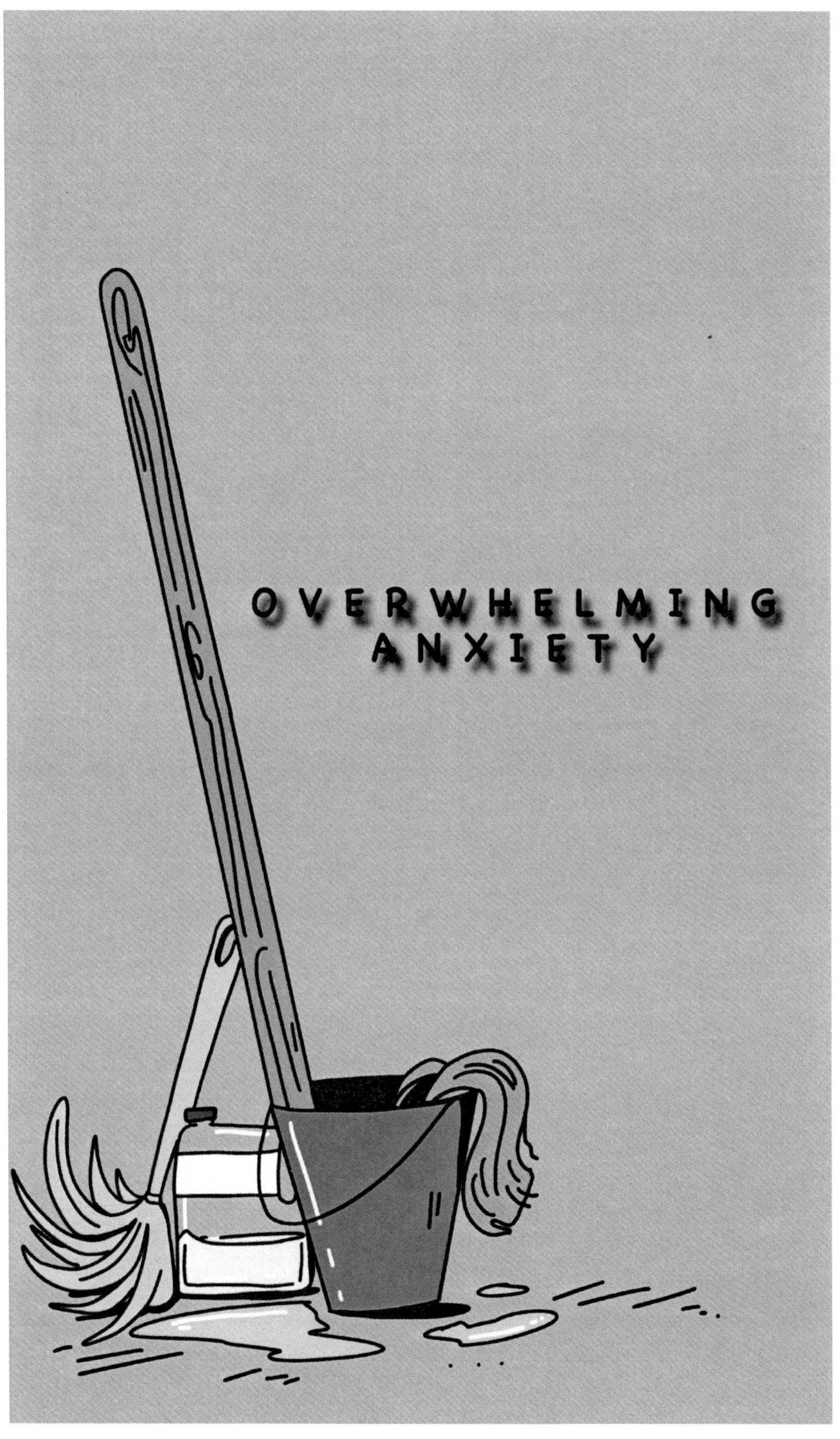

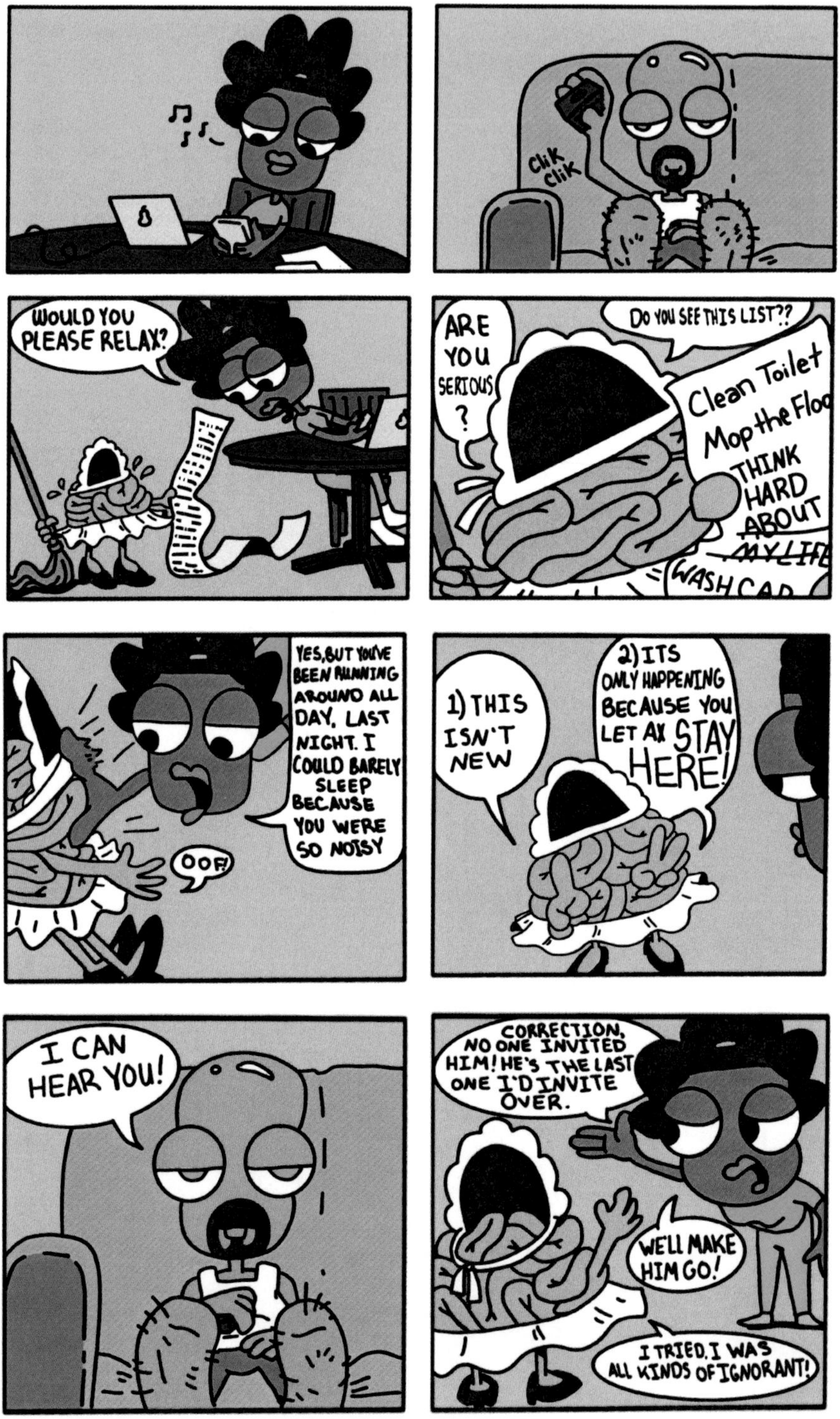
CliK CliK
WOULD YOU PLEASE RELAX?
ARE YOU SERIOUS ?
DO YOU SEE THIS LIST??
Clean Toilet
Mop the Floo
THINK HARD ABOUT MY LIFE
WASH CAR
YES, BUT YOU'VE BEEN RUNNING AROUND ALL DAY, LAST NIGHT. I COULD BARELY SLEEP BECAUSE YOU WERE SO NOISY
OOF!
1) THIS ISN'T NEW
2) ITS ONLY HAPPENING BECAUSE YOU LET AX STAY HERE!
I CAN HEAR YOU!
CORRECTION, NO ONE INVITED HIM! HE'S THE LAST ONE I'D INVITE OVER.
WE'LL MAKE HIM GO!
I TRIED. I WAS ALL KINDS OF IGNORANT!

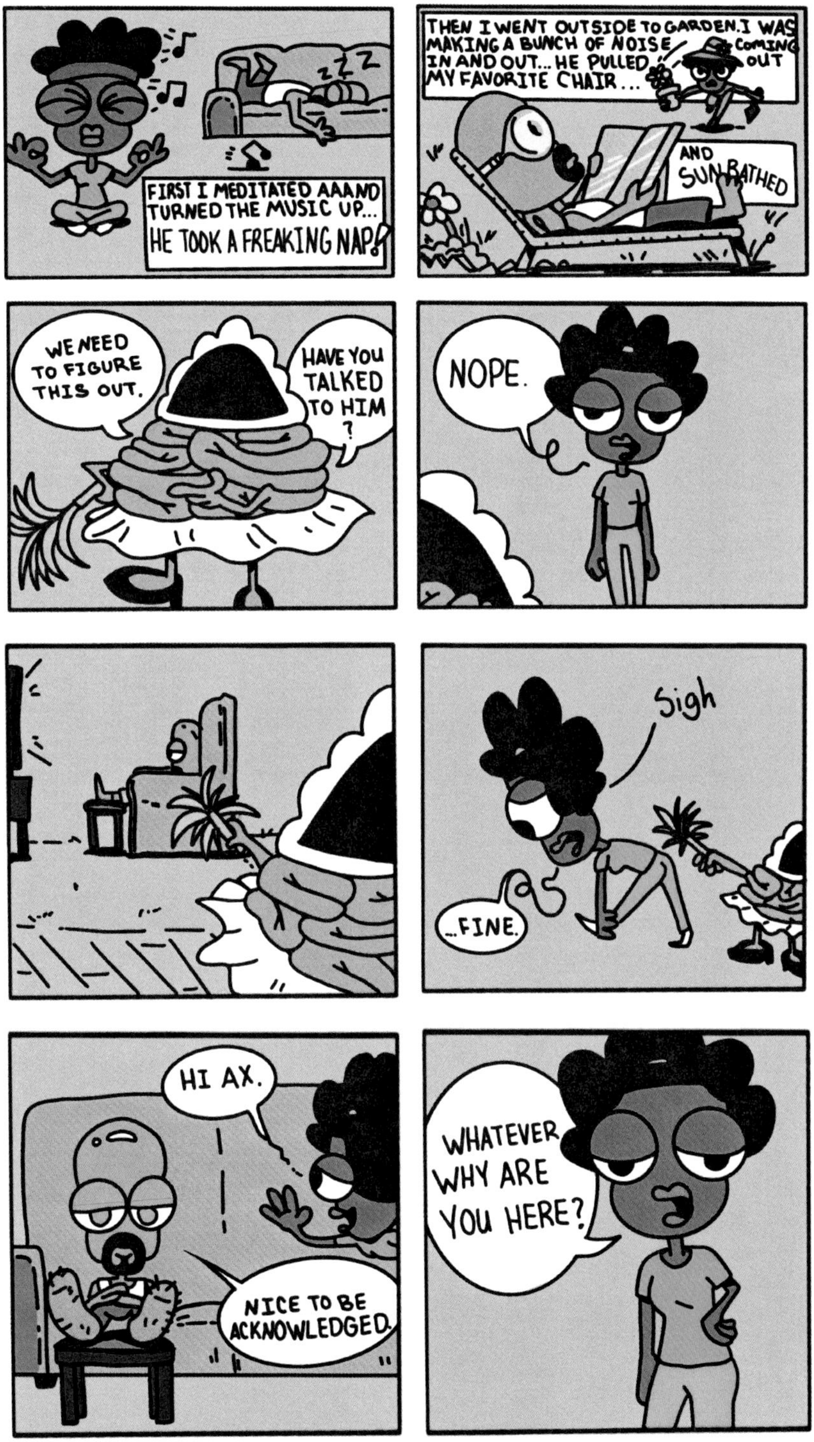
FIRST I MEDITATED AAAND TURNED THE MUSIC UP...
HE TOOK A FREAKING NAP!
THEN I WENT OUTSIDE TO GARDEN. I WAS MAKING A BUNCH OF NOISE COMING IN AND OUT... HE PULLED OUT MY FAVORITE CHAIR...
AND SUNBATHED
WE NEED TO FIGURE THIS OUT.
HAVE YOU TALKED TO HIM?
NOPE.
Sigh
...FINE.
HI AX.
NICE TO BE ACKNOWLEDGED.
WHATEVER WHY ARE YOU HERE?

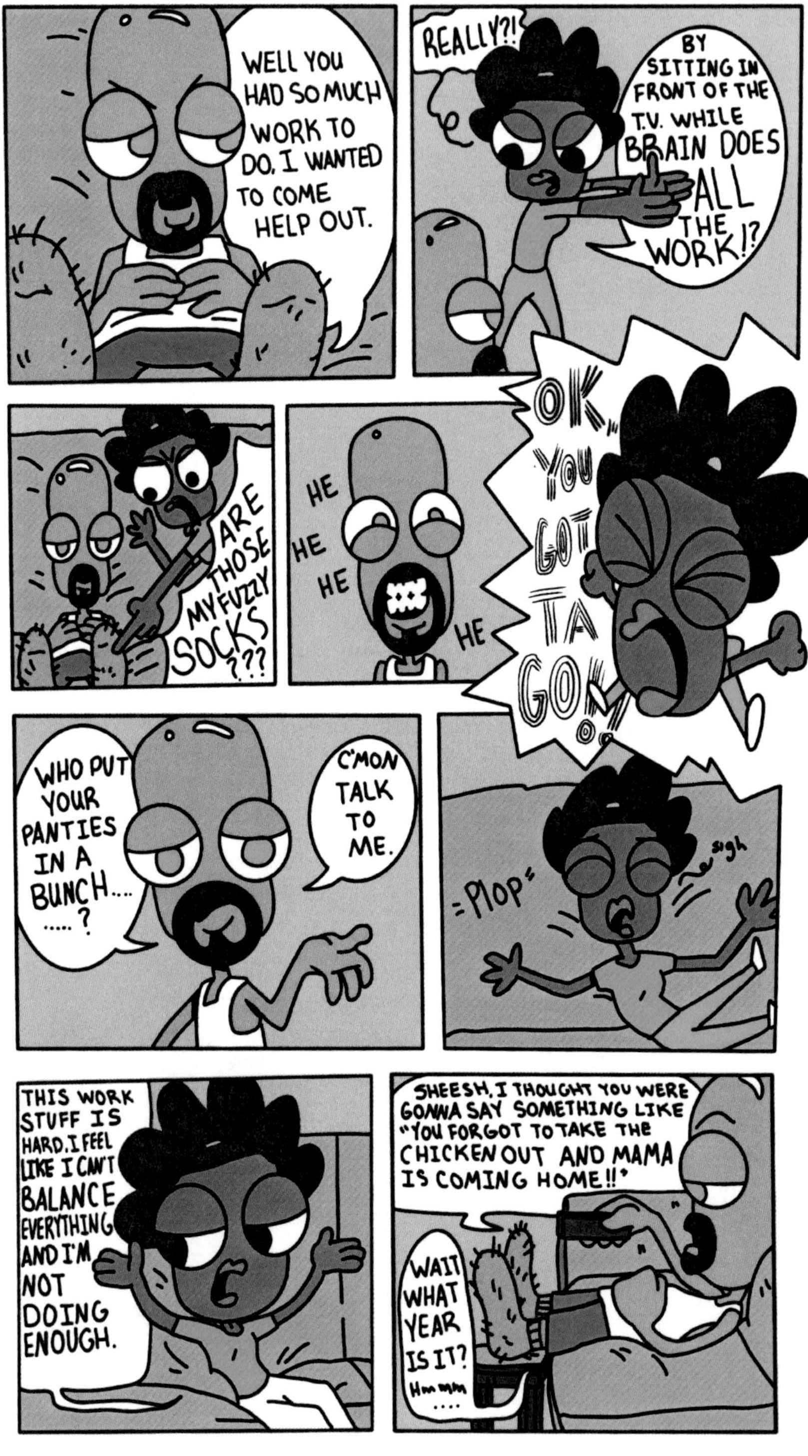

WELL YOU HAD SO MUCH WORK TO DO, I WANTED TO COME HELP OUT.
REALLY?!
BY SITTING IN FRONT OF THE T.V. WHILE BRAIN DOES ALL THE WORK!?
ARE THOSE MY FUZZY SOCKS???
HE HE HE HE
OK, YOU GOTTA GO!!
WHO PUT YOUR PANTIES IN A BUNCH.... .....?
C'MON TALK TO ME.
PLOP
sigh
THIS WORK STUFF IS HARD. I FEEL LIKE I CAN'T BALANCE EVERYTHING AND I'M NOT DOING ENOUGH.
SHEESH, I THOUGHT YOU WERE GONNA SAY SOMETHING LIKE "YOU FORGOT TO TAKE THE CHICKEN OUT AND MAMA IS COMING HOME!!"
WAIT WHAT YEAR IS IT? Hmmm ....

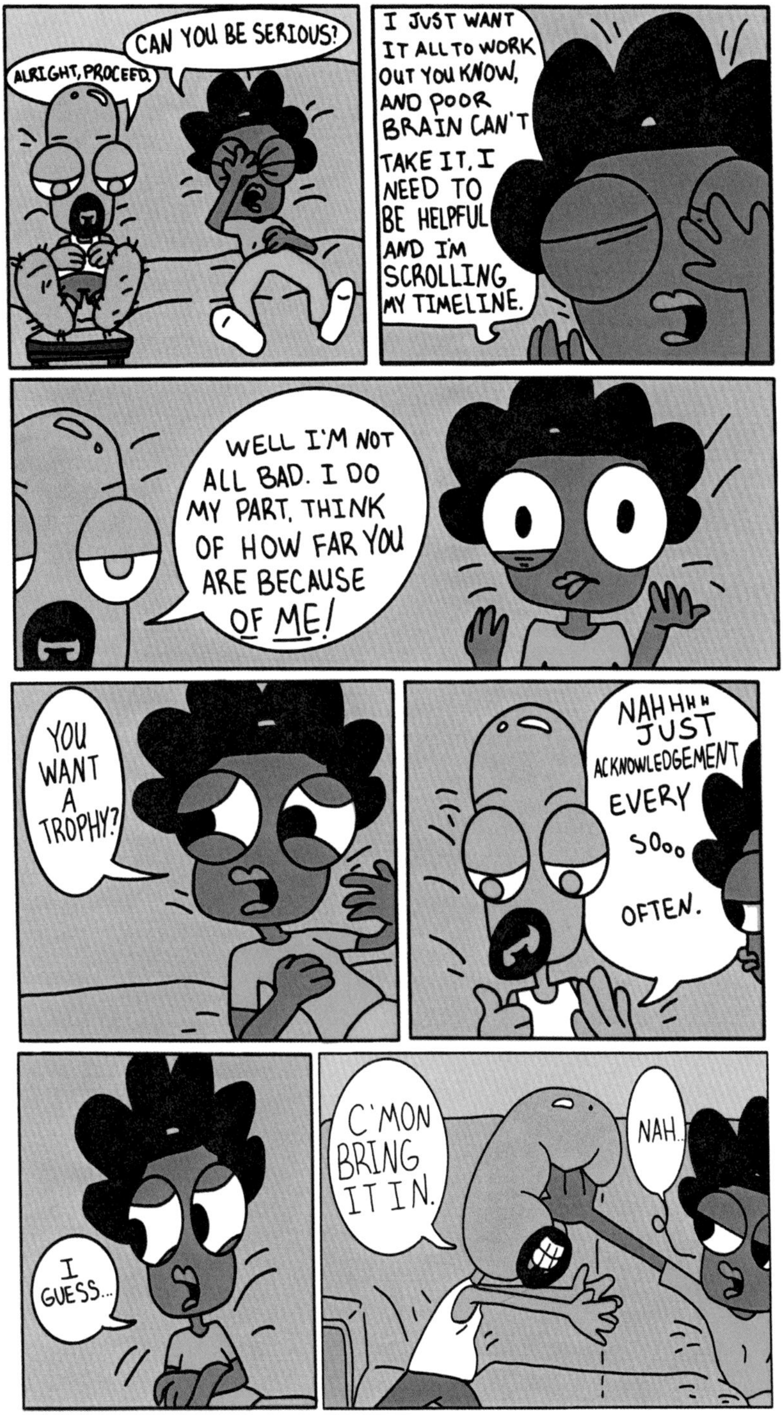
CAN YOU BE SERIOUS?
ALRIGHT, PROCEED.
I JUST WANT IT ALL TO WORK OUT YOU KNOW, AND POOR BRAIN CAN'T TAKE IT. I NEED TO BE HELPFUL AND I'M SCROLLING MY TIMELINE.
WELL I'M NOT ALL BAD. I DO MY PART. THINK OF HOW FAR YOU ARE BECAUSE OF ME!
YOU WANT A TROPHY?
NAHHHH JUST ACKNOWLEDGEMENT EVERY SOoo OFTEN.
I GUESS...
C'MON BRING IT IN.
NAH..

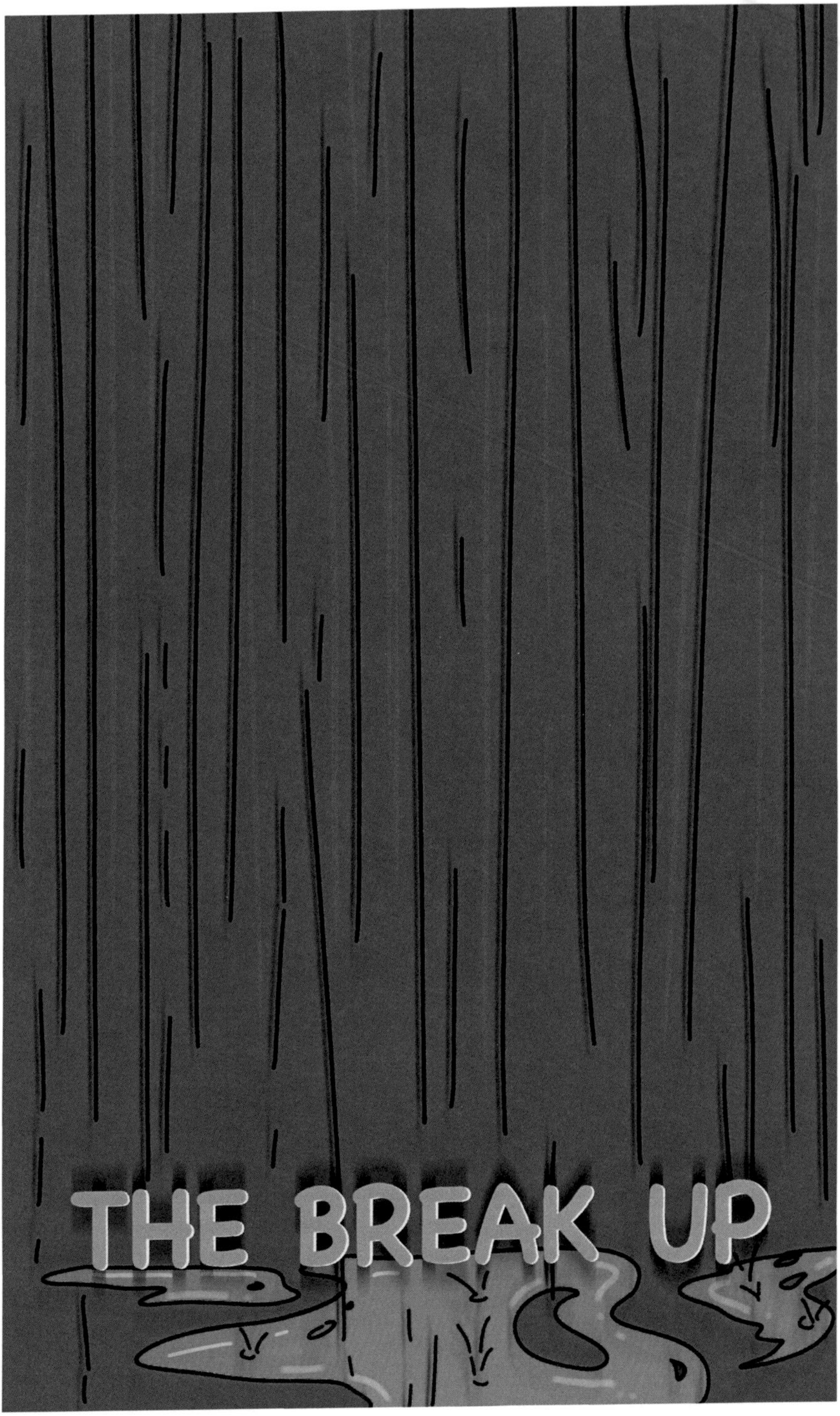
THE BREAK UP

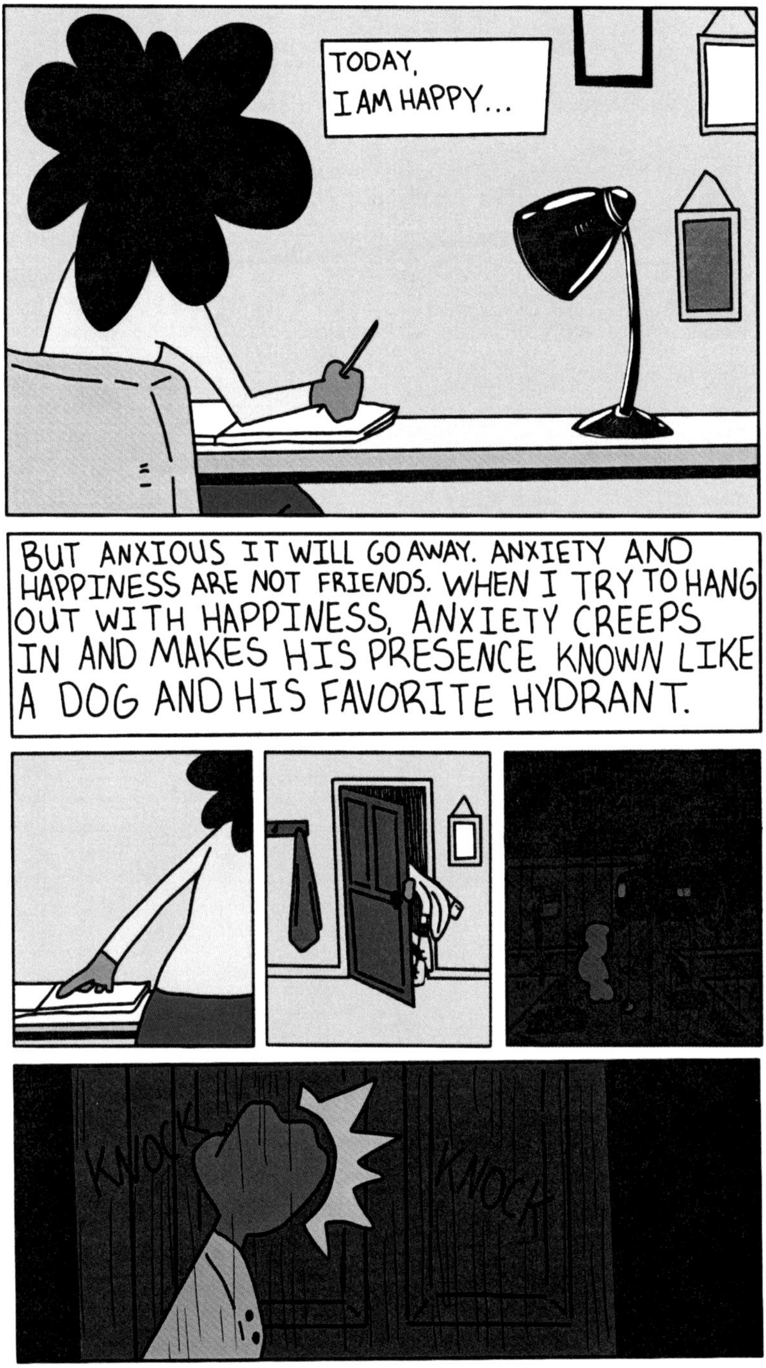
TODAY,
I AM HAPPY...
BUT ANXIOUS IT WILL GO AWAY. ANXIETY AND HAPPINESS ARE NOT FRIENDS. WHEN I TRY TO HANG OUT WITH HAPPINESS, ANXIETY CREEPS IN AND MAKES HIS PRESENCE KNOWN LIKE A DOG AND HIS FAVORITE HYDRANT.
KNOCK
KNOCK

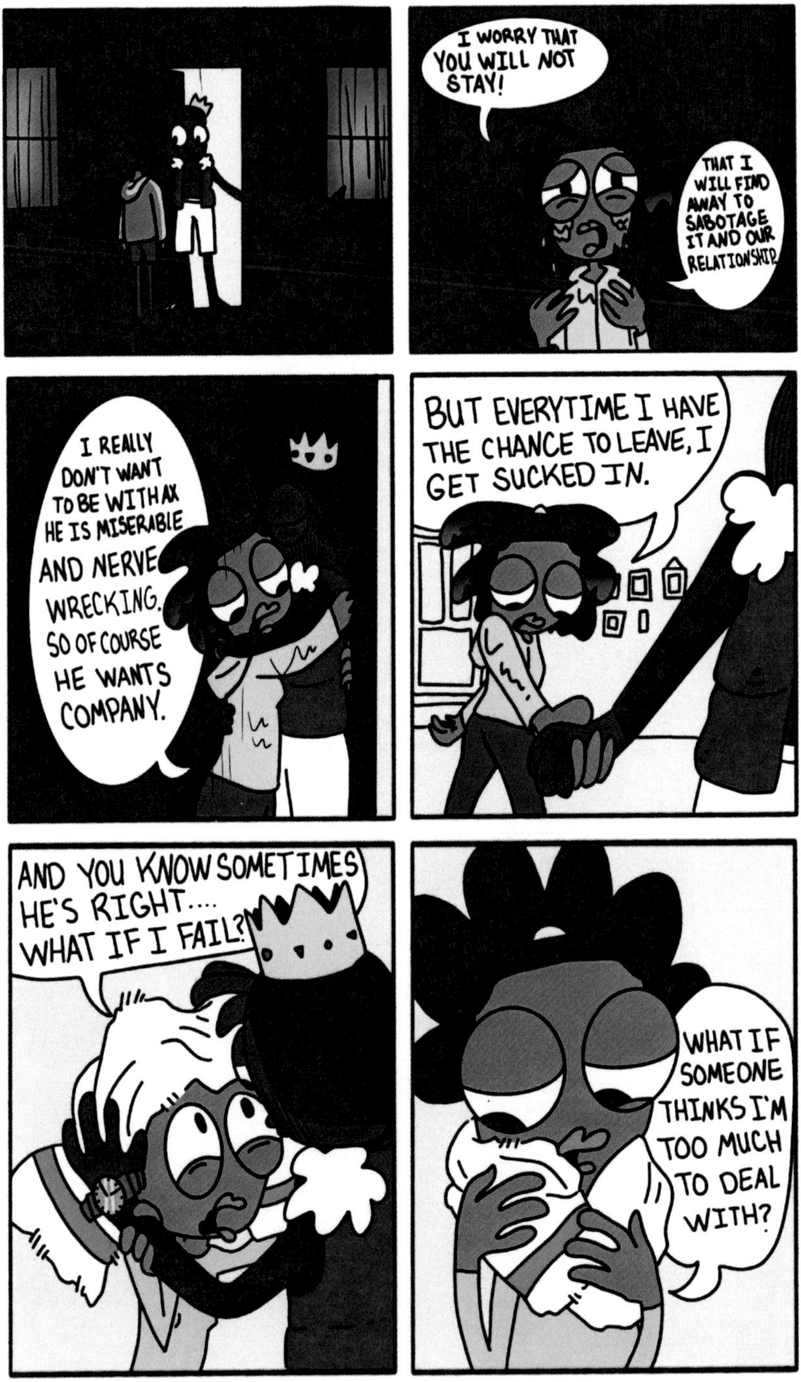
I WORRY THAT YOU WILL NOT STAY!
THAT I WILL FIND AWAY TO SABOTAGE IT AND OUR RELATIONSHIP.
I REALLY DON'T WANT TO BE WITH AX HE IS MISERABLE AND NERVE WRECKING. SO OF COURSE HE WANTS COMPANY.
BUT EVERYTIME I HAVE THE CHANCE TO LEAVE, I GET SUCKED IN.
AND YOU KNOW SOMETIMES HE'S RIGHT.... WHAT IF I FAIL?
WHAT IF SOMEONE THINKS I'M TOO MUCH TO DEAL WITH?

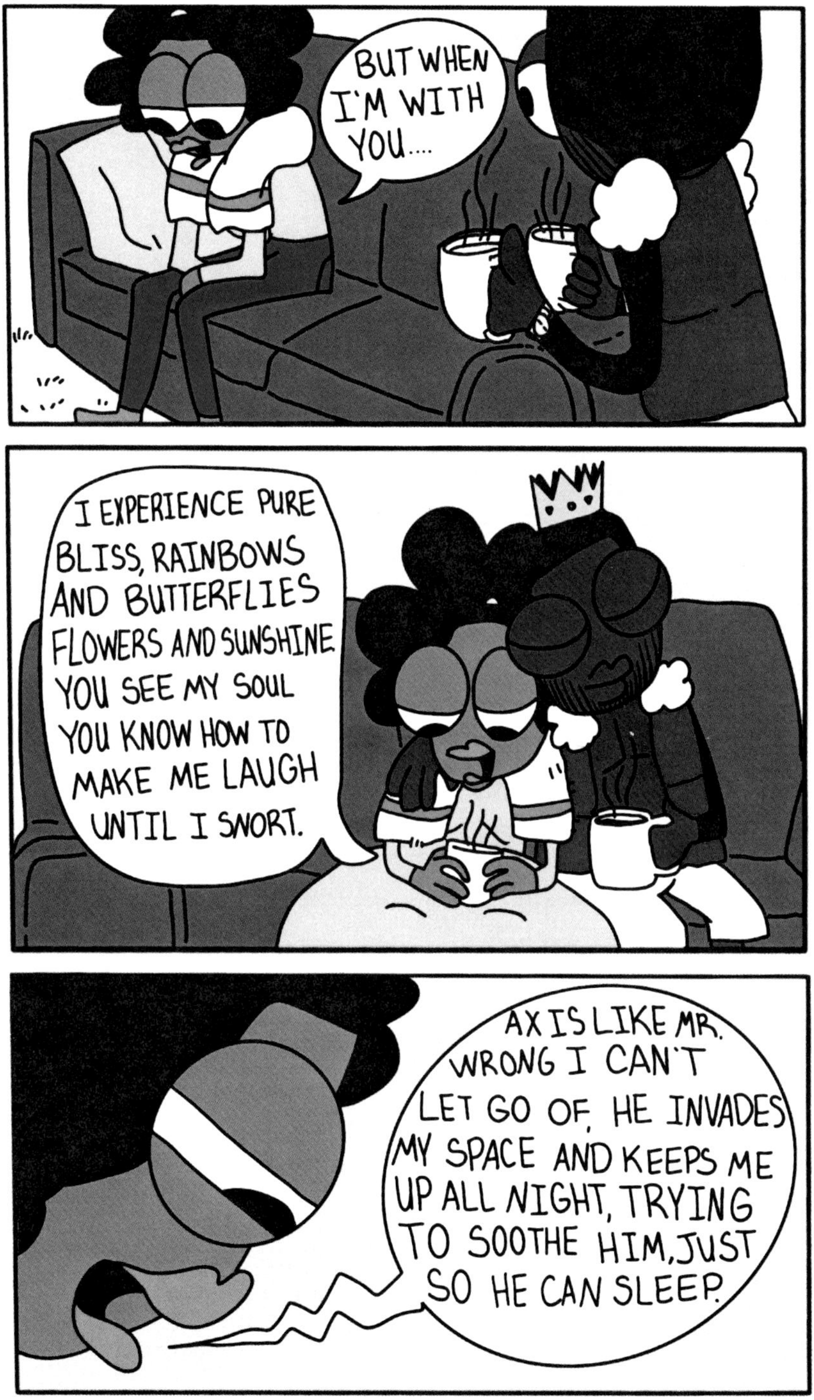
BUT WHEN I'M WITH YOU....
I EXPERIENCE PURE BLISS, RAINBOWS AND BUTTERFLIES FLOWERS AND SUNSHINE YOU SEE MY SOUL YOU KNOW HOW TO MAKE ME LAUGH UNTIL I SNORT.
AX IS LIKE MR. WRONG I CAN'T LET GO OF, HE INVADES MY SPACE AND KEEPS ME UP ALL NIGHT, TRYING TO SOOTHE HIM, JUST SO HE CAN SLEEP.

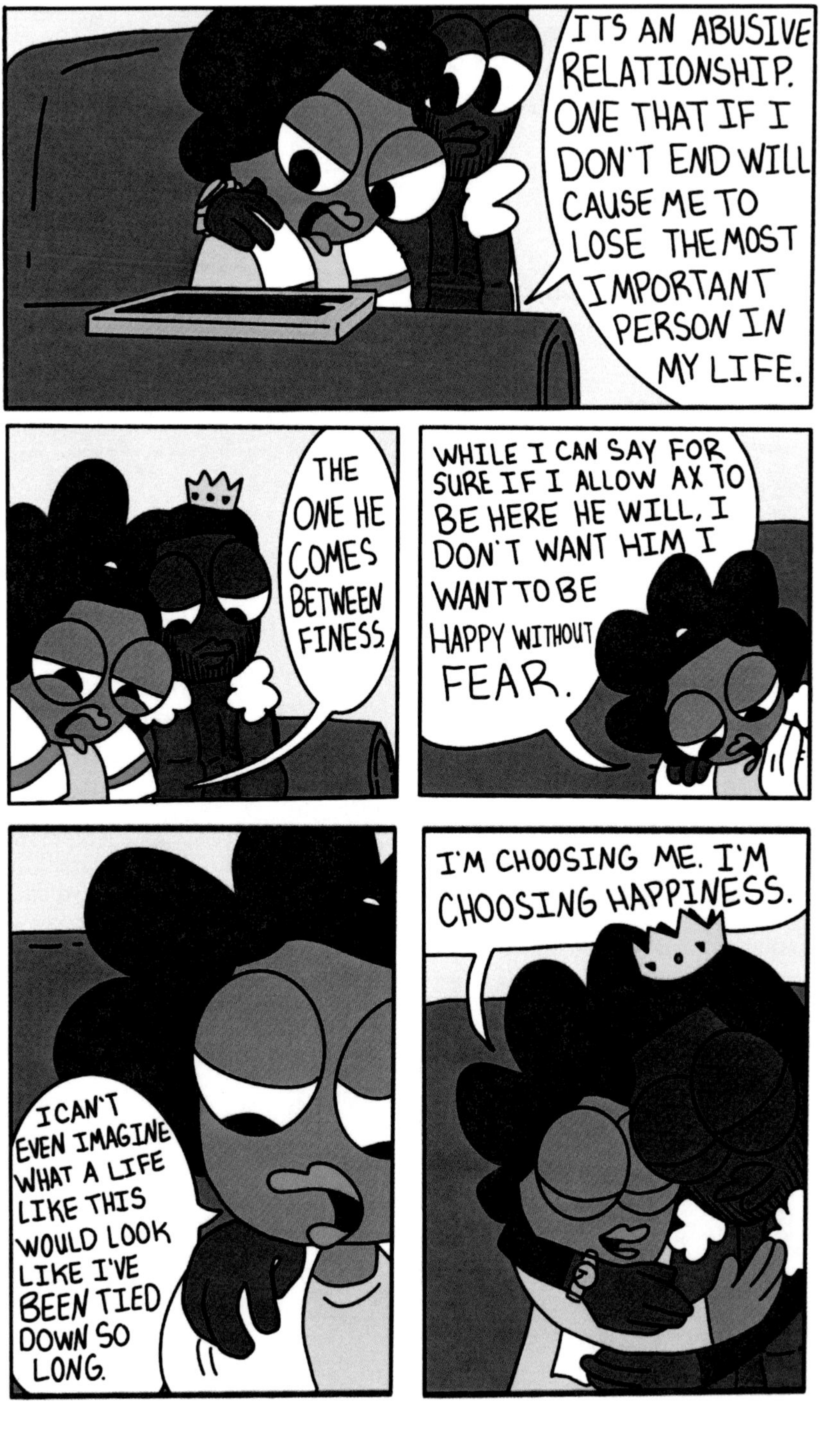
ITS AN ABUSIVE RELATIONSHIP. ONE THAT IF I DON'T END WILL CAUSE ME TO LOSE THE MOST IMPORTANT PERSON IN MY LIFE.
THE ONE HE COMES BETWEEN FINESS.
WHILE I CAN SAY FOR SURE IF I ALLOW AX TO BE HERE HE WILL, I DON'T WANT HIM I WANT TO BE HAPPY WITHOUT FEAR.
I CAN'T EVEN IMAGINE WHAT A LIFE LIKE THIS WOULD LOOK LIKE I'VE BEEN TIED DOWN SO LONG.
I'M CHOOSING ME. I'M CHOOSING HAPPINESS.

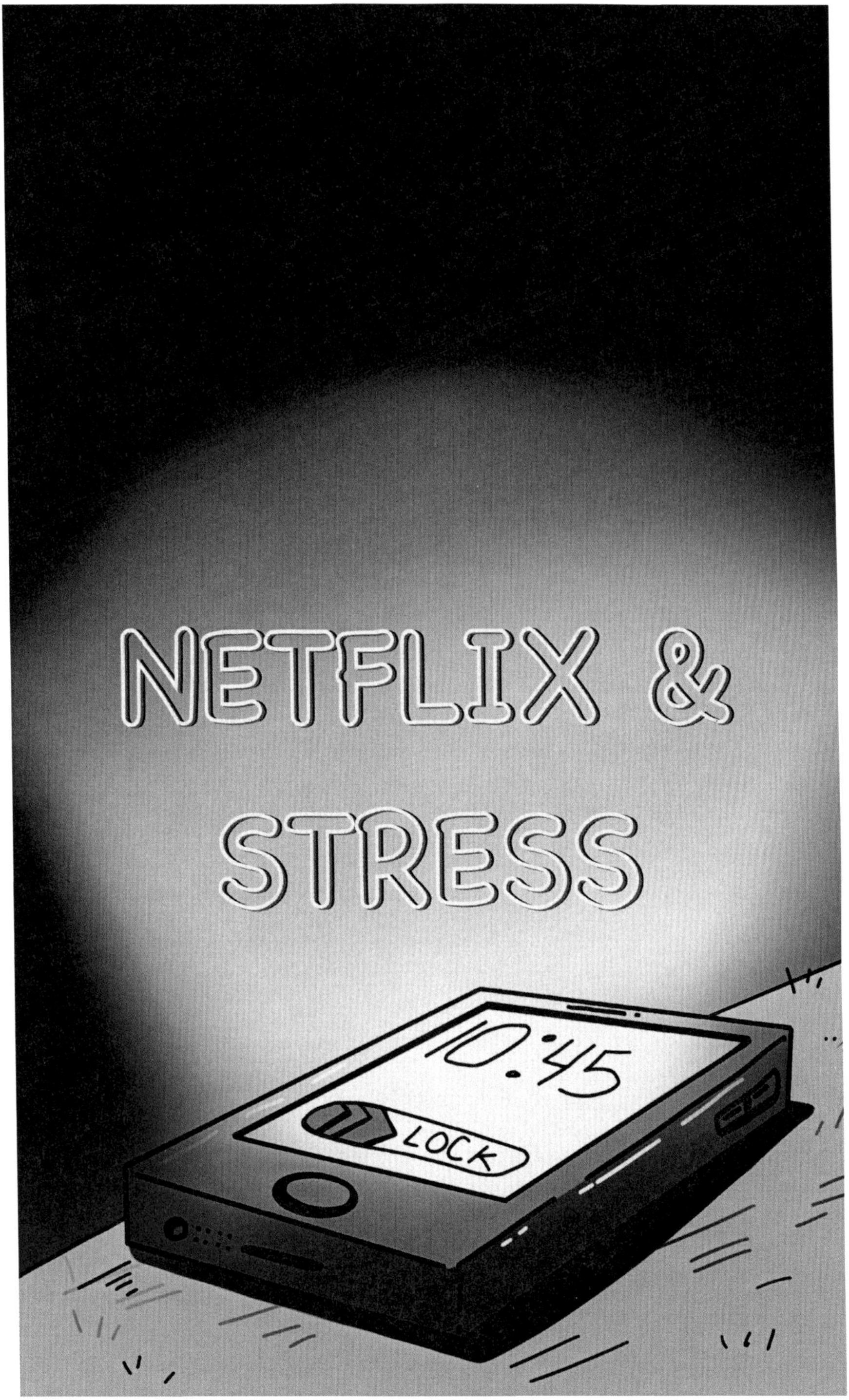
NETFLIX &
STRESS
10:45
LOCK

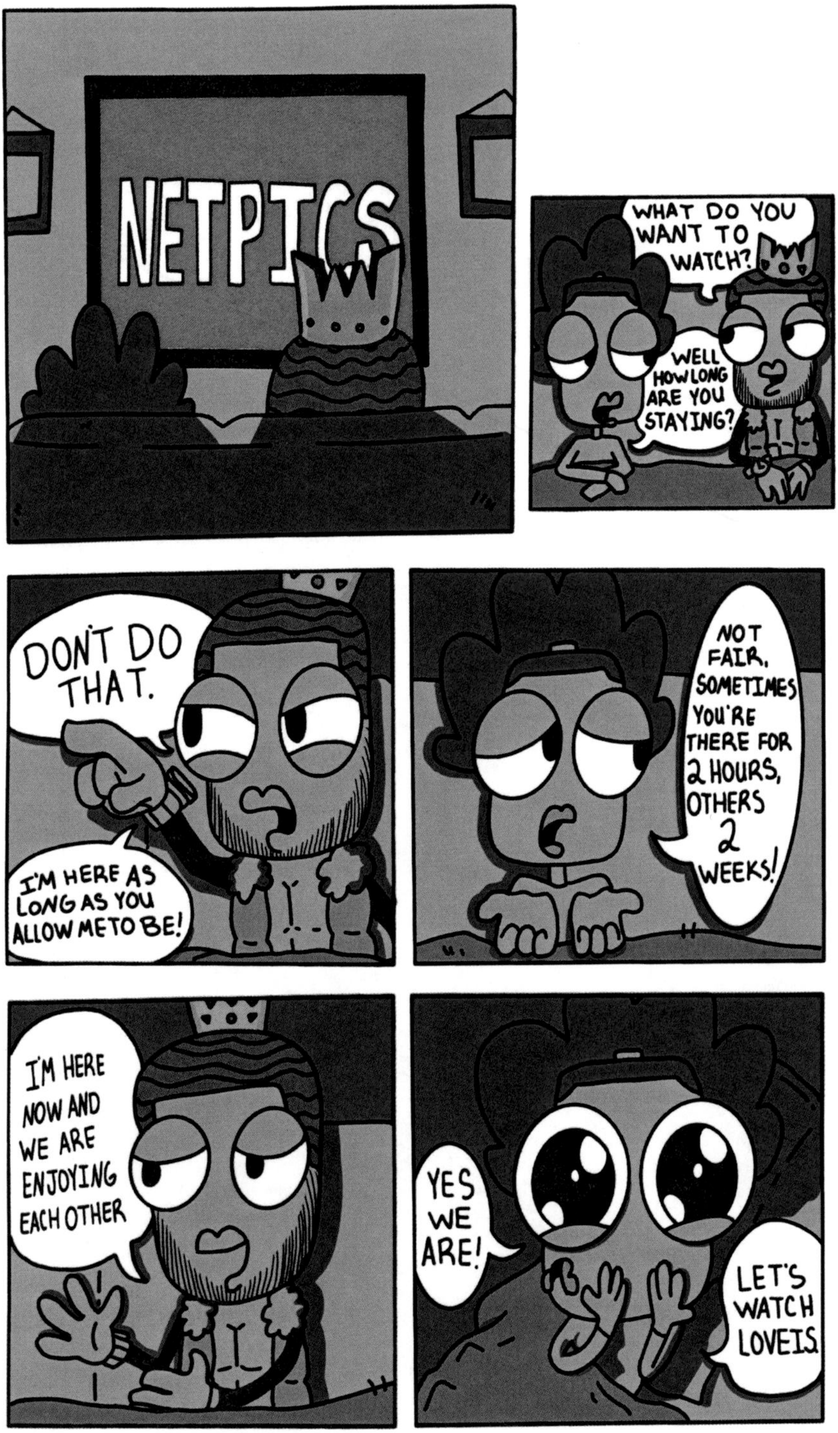
NETPICS
WHAT DO YOU WANT TO WATCH?
WELL HOW LONG ARE YOU STAYING?
DON'T DO THAT.
I'M HERE AS LONG AS YOU ALLOW ME TO BE!
NOT FAIR, SOMETIMES YOU'RE THERE FOR 2 HOURS, OTHERS 2 WEEKS!
I'M HERE NOW AND WE ARE ENJOYING EACH OTHER
YES WE ARE!
LET'S WATCH LOVE IS.

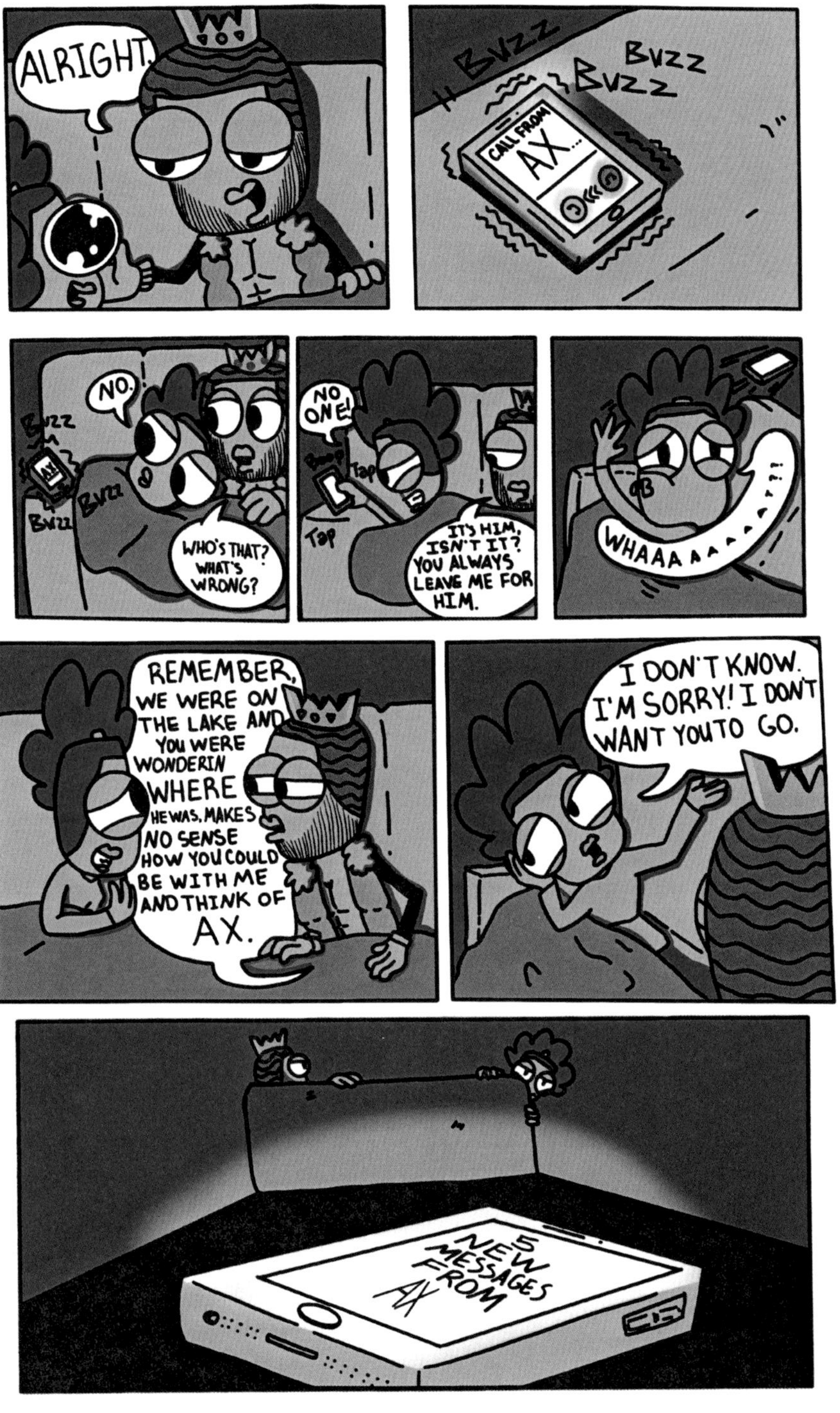
ALRIGHT.
BUZZ
BUZZ
BUZZ
CALL FROM AX...
NO.
BUZZ
BUZZ
BUZZ
WHO'S THAT? WHAT'S WRONG?
NO ONE!
Boop
Tap
Tap
IT'S HIM, ISN'T IT? YOU ALWAYS LEAVE ME FOR HIM.
WHAAAAAAAA??!
REMEMBER, WE WERE ON THE LAKE AND YOU WERE WONDERIN WHERE HE WAS, MAKES NO SENSE HOW YOU COULD BE WITH ME AND THINK OF AX.
I DON'T KNOW. I'M SORRY! I DON'T WANT YOU TO GO.
5 NEW MESSAGES FROM AX

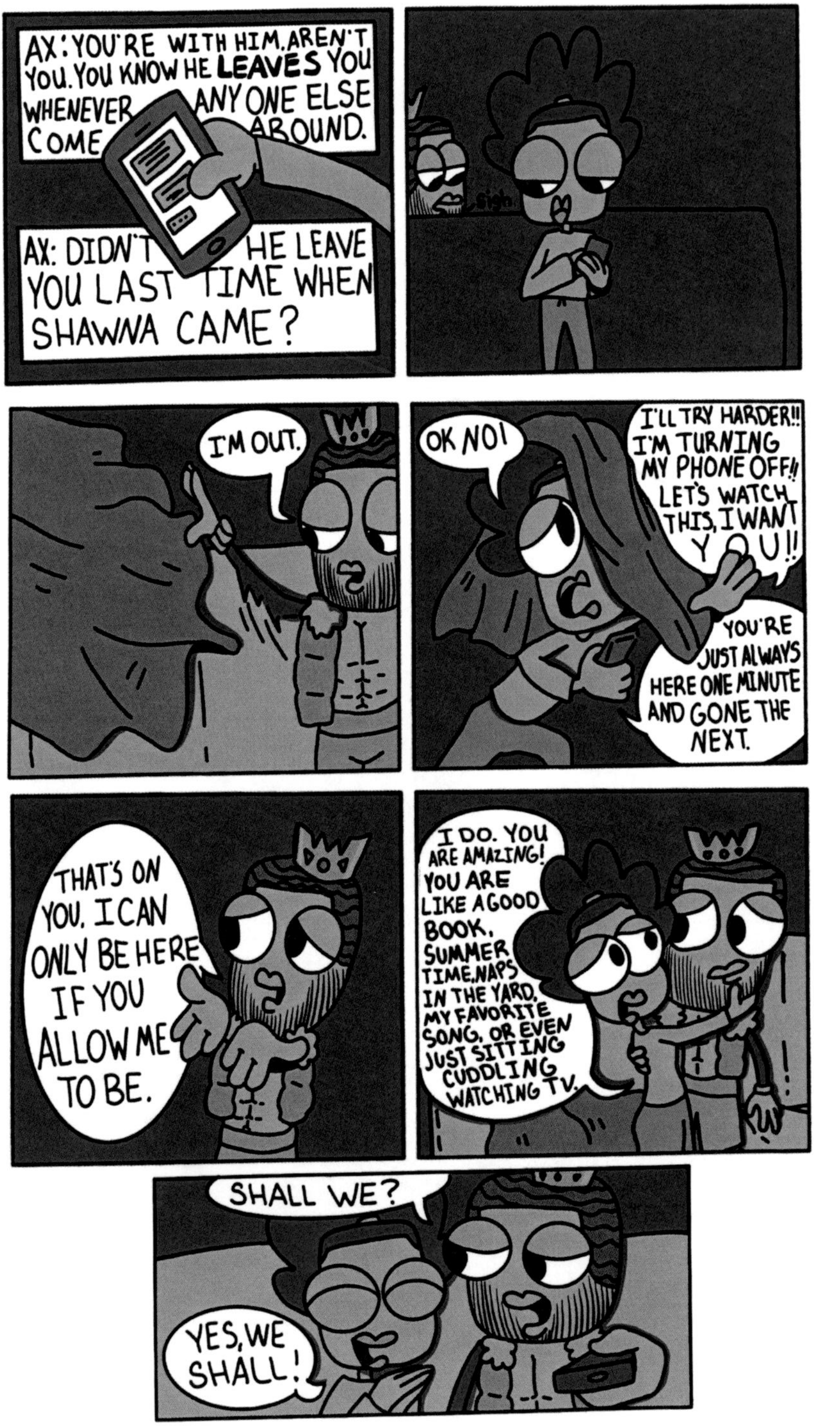

AX: YOU'RE WITH HIM, AREN'T YOU. YOU KNOW HE LEAVES YOU WHENEVER ANY ONE ELSE COME AROUND.
AX: DIDN'T HE LEAVE YOU LAST TIME WHEN SHAWNA CAME?
Sigh
I'M OUT.
OK NO!
I'LL TRY HARDER!! I'M TURNING MY PHONE OFF!! LET'S WATCH THIS, I WANT YOU!!
YOU'RE JUST ALWAYS HERE ONE MINUTE AND GONE THE NEXT.
THAT'S ON YOU. I CAN ONLY BE HERE IF YOU ALLOW ME TO BE.
I DO. YOU ARE AMAZING! YOU ARE LIKE A GOOD BOOK, SUMMER TIME, NAPS IN THE YARD, MY FAVORITE SONG, OR EVEN JUST SITTING CUDDLING WATCHING TV.
SHALL WE?
YES, WE SHALL!

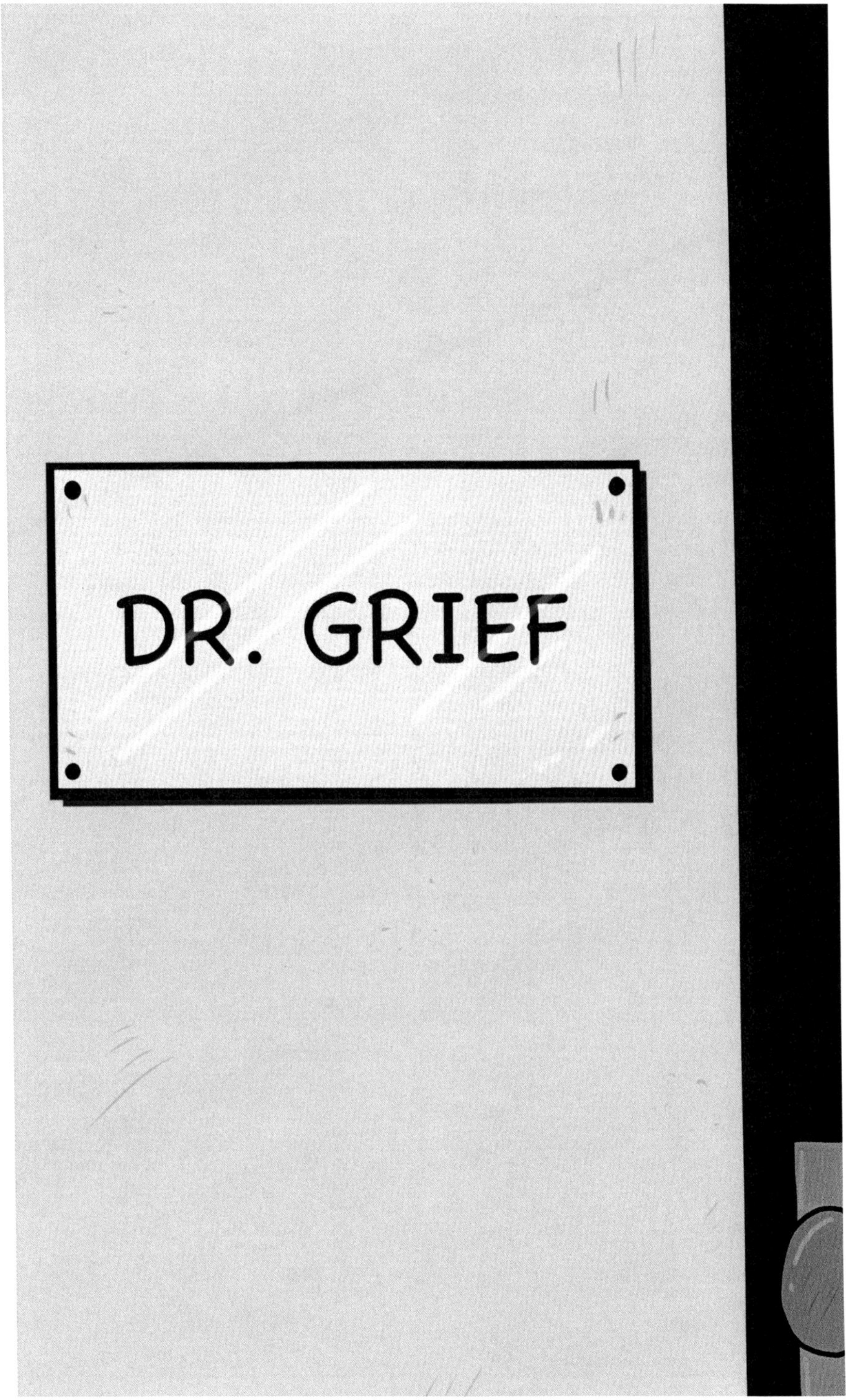
DR. GRIEF

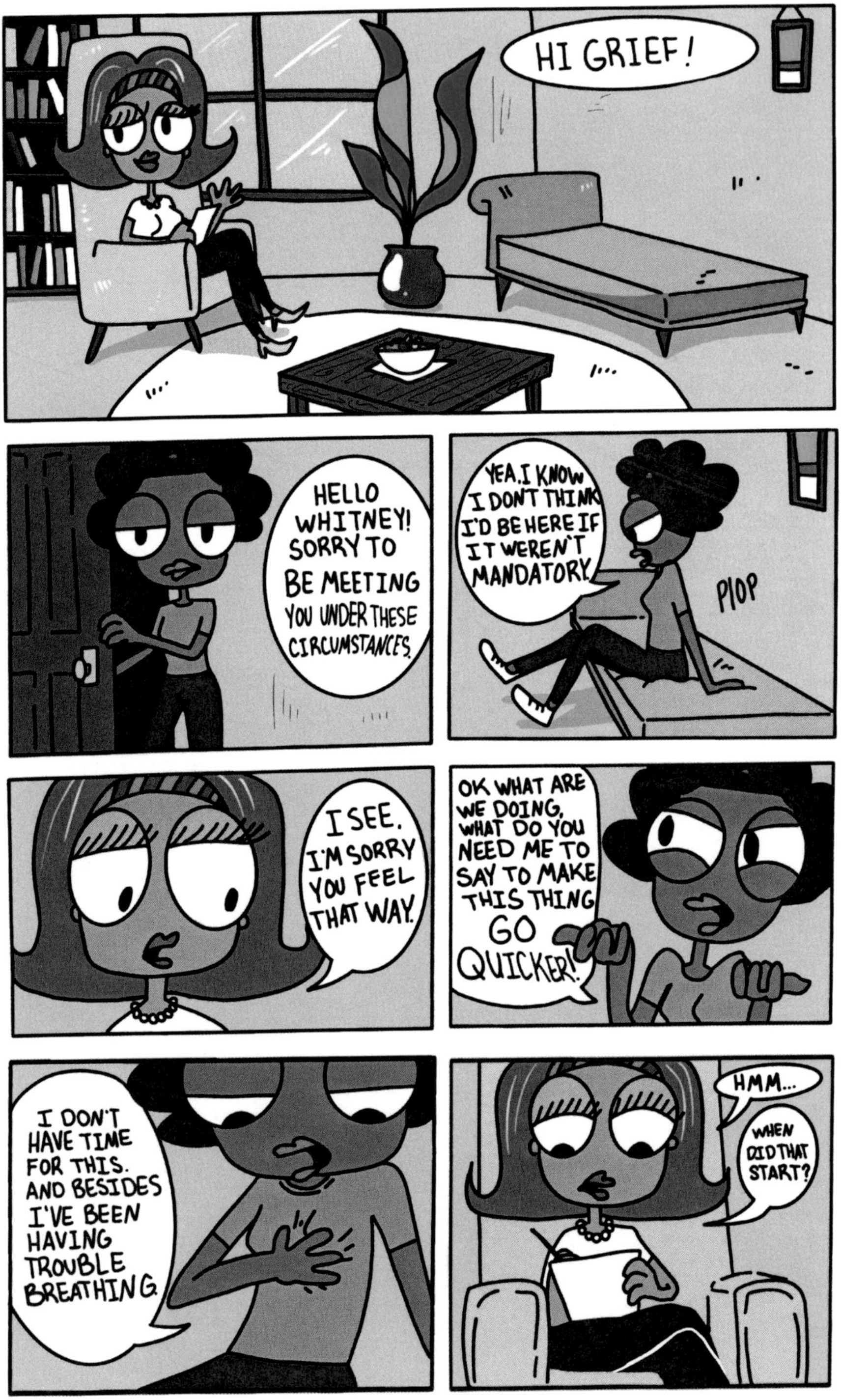

HI GRIEF!
HELLO WHITNEY! SORRY TO BE MEETING YOU UNDER THESE CIRCUMSTANCES.
YEA, I KNOW I DON'T THINK I'D BE HERE IF IT WEREN'T MANDATORY.
PLOP
I SEE. I'M SORRY YOU FEEL THAT WAY.
OK WHAT ARE WE DOING, WHAT DO YOU NEED ME TO SAY TO MAKE THIS THING GO QUICKER!
I DON'T HAVE TIME FOR THIS. AND BESIDES I'VE BEEN HAVING TROUBLE BREATHING.
HMM...
WHEN DID THAT START?

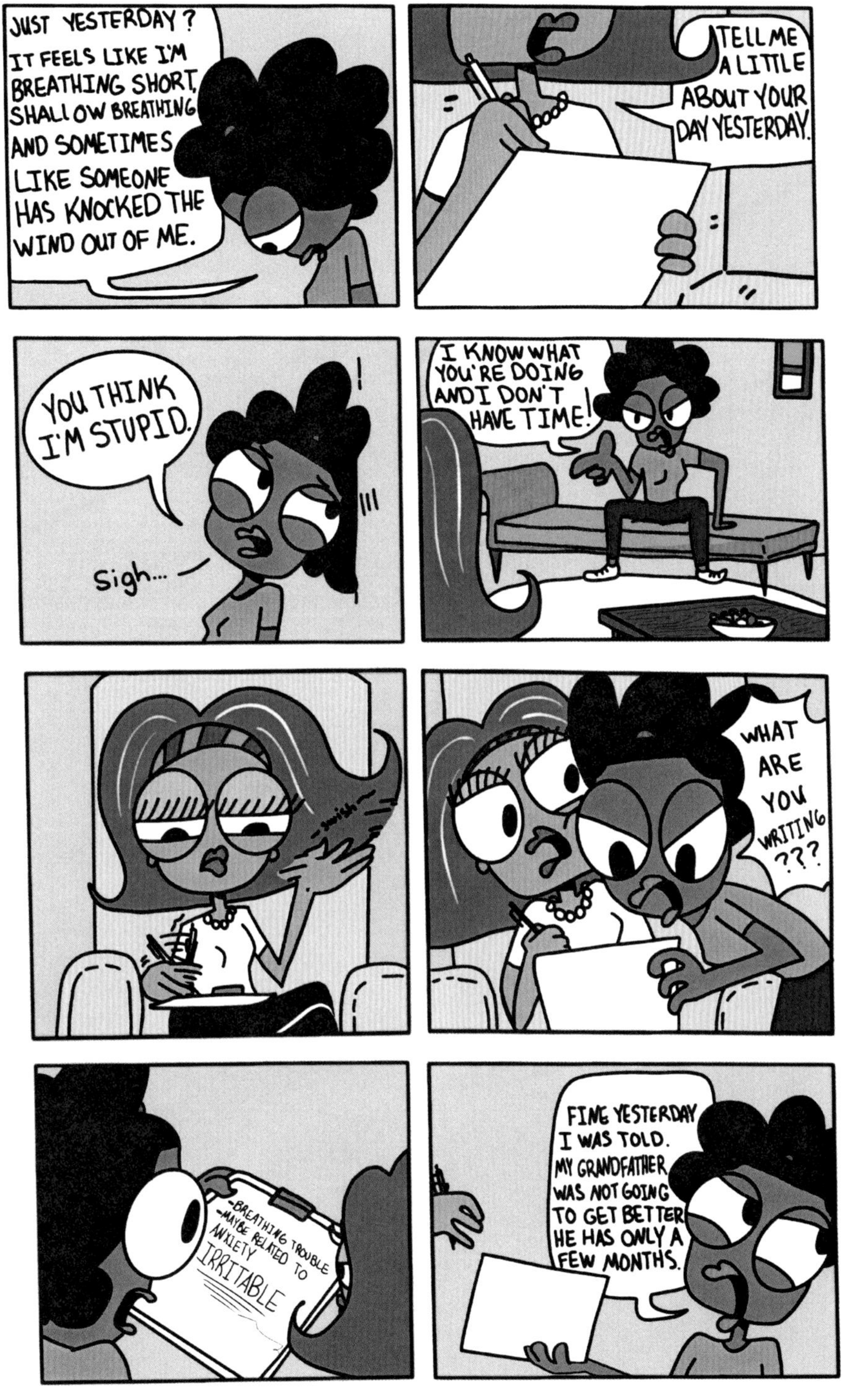
JUST YESTERDAY? IT FEELS LIKE I'M BREATHING SHORT, SHALLOW BREATHING AND SOMETIMES LIKE SOMEONE HAS KNOCKED THE WIND OUT OF ME.
TELL ME A LITTLE ABOUT YOUR DAY YESTERDAY.
YOU THINK I'M STUPID.
Sigh...
I KNOW WHAT YOU'RE DOING AND I DON'T HAVE TIME!
WHAT ARE YOU WRITING???
-BREATHING TROUBLE
-MAYBE RELATED TO ANXIETY
IRRITABLE
FINE YESTERDAY I WAS TOLD. MY GRANDFATHER WAS NOT GOING TO GET BETTER HE HAS ONLY A FEW MONTHS.

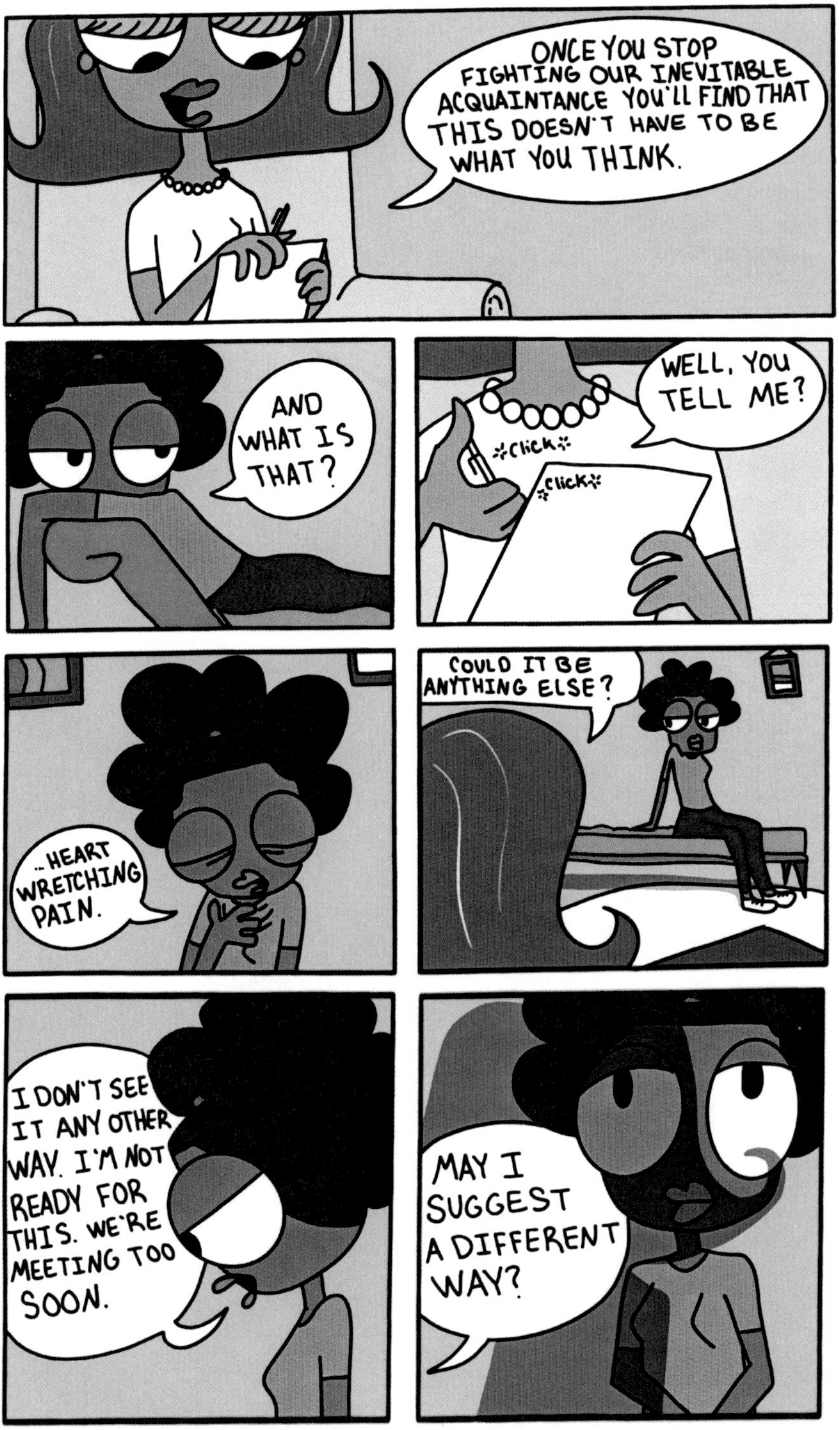
ONCE YOU STOP FIGHTING OUR INEVITABLE ACQUAINTANCE YOU'LL FIND THAT THIS DOESN'T HAVE TO BE WHAT YOU THINK.
AND WHAT IS THAT?
WELL, YOU TELL ME?
click
click
...HEART WRETCHING PAIN.
COULD IT BE ANYTHING ELSE?
I DON'T SEE IT ANY OTHER WAY. I'M NOT READY FOR THIS. WE'RE MEETING TOO SOON.
MAY I SUGGEST A DIFFERENT WAY?

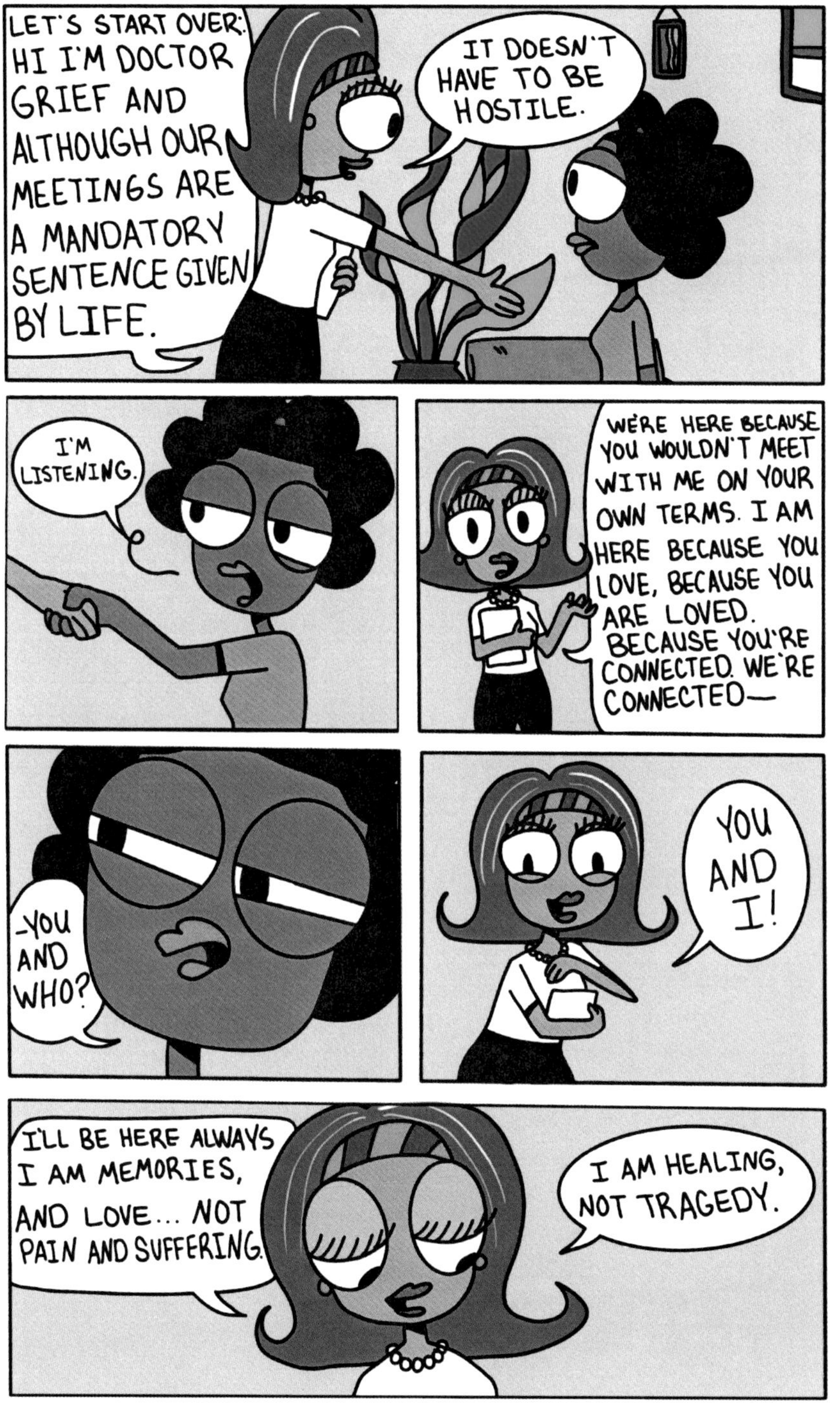
LET'S START OVER: HI I'M DOCTOR GRIEF AND ALTHOUGH OUR MEETINGS ARE A MANDATORY SENTENCE GIVEN BY LIFE.
IT DOESN'T HAVE TO BE HOSTILE.
I'M LISTENING.
WE'RE HERE BECAUSE YOU WOULDN'T MEET WITH ME ON YOUR OWN TERMS. I AM HERE BECAUSE YOU LOVE, BECAUSE YOU ARE LOVED. BECAUSE YOU'RE CONNECTED. WE'RE CONNECTED—
-YOU AND WHO?
YOU AND I!
I'LL BE HERE ALWAYS I AM MEMORIES, AND LOVE... NOT PAIN AND SUFFERING.
I AM HEALING, NOT TRAGEDY.

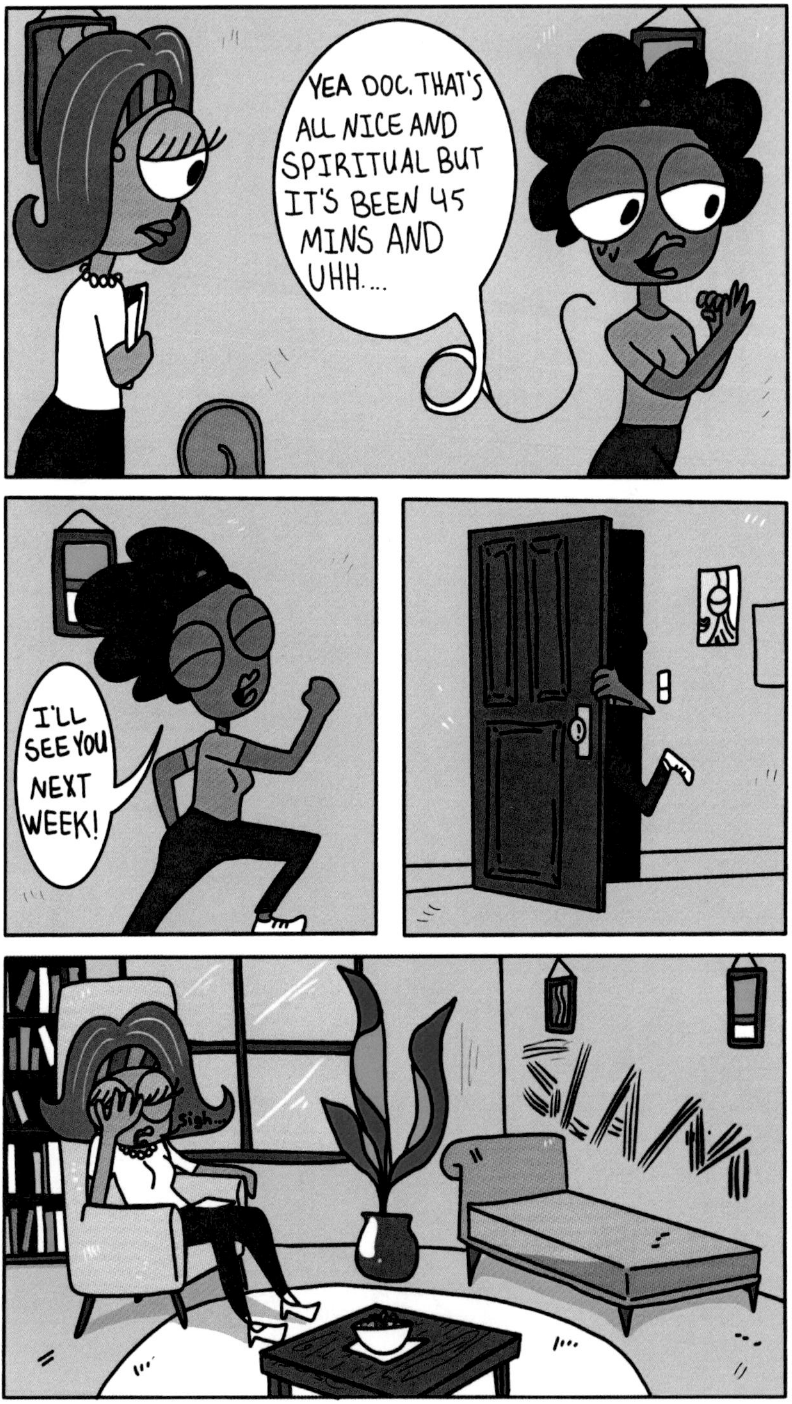
YEA DOC. THAT'S ALL NICE AND SPIRITUAL BUT IT'S BEEN 45 MINS AND UHH....
I'LL SEE YOU NEXT WEEK!
SIGH...
SLAM!

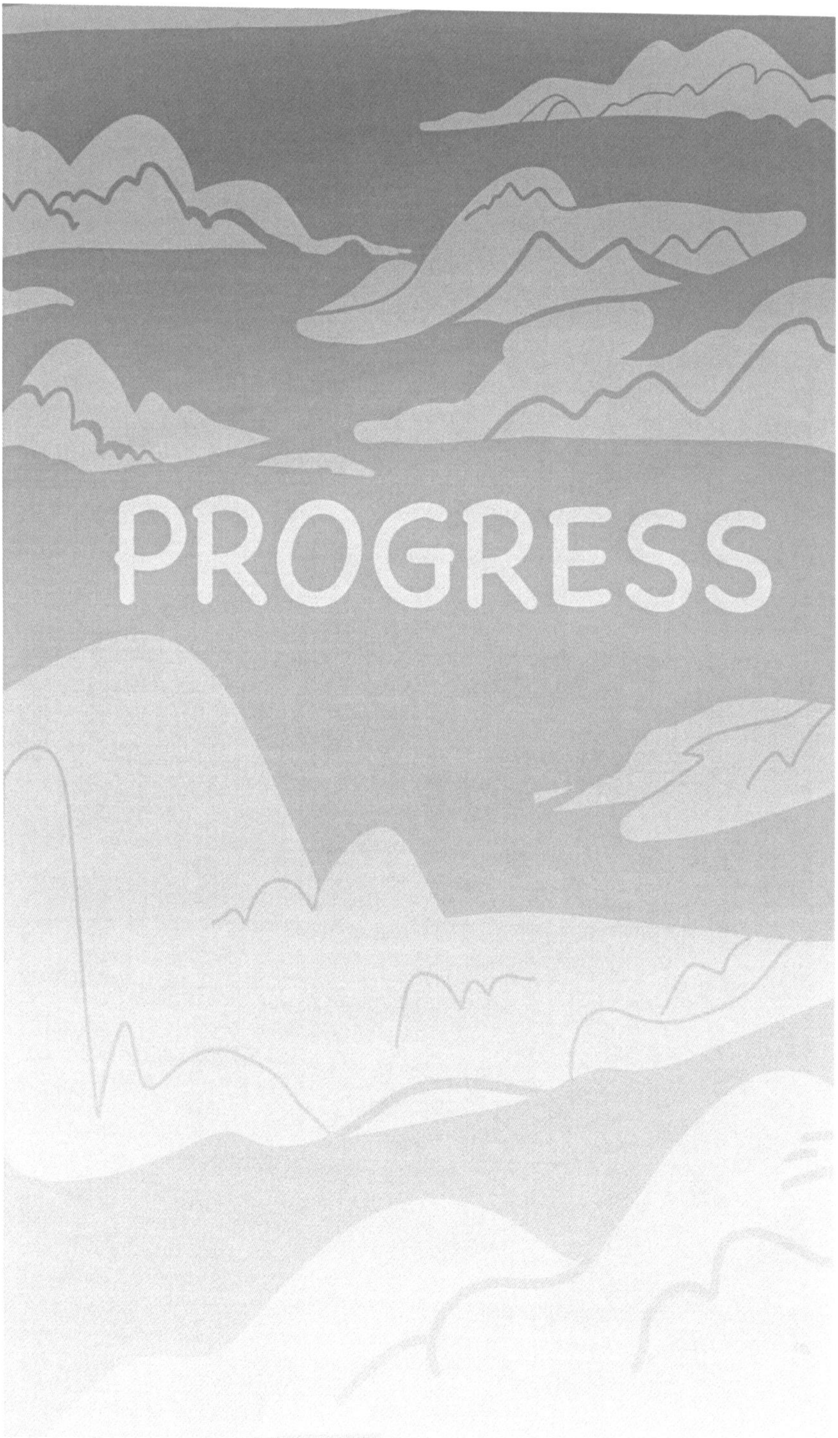
PROGRESS

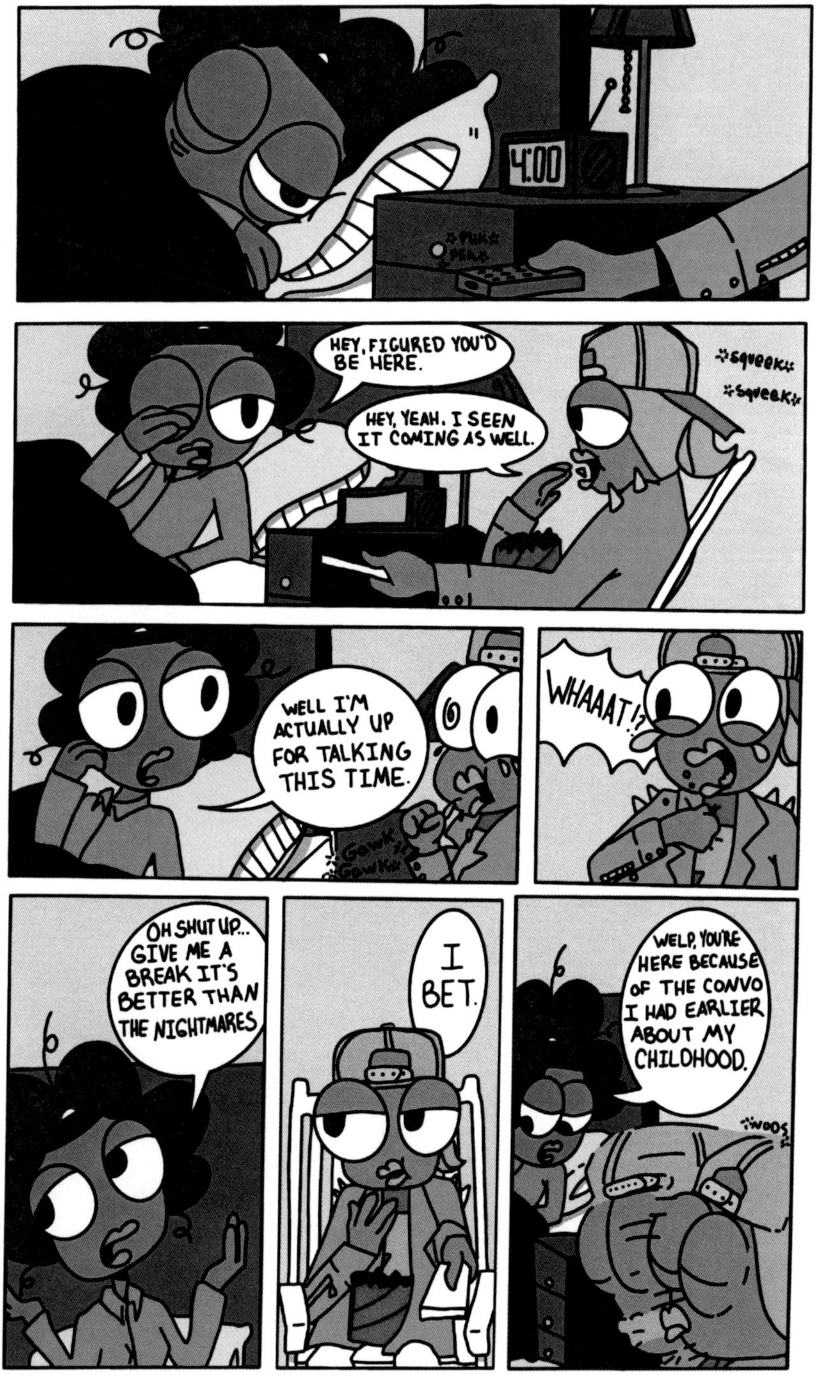
4:00
HEY, FIGURED YOU'D BE HERE.
HEY, YEAH. I SEEN IT COMING AS WELL.
squeek
squeek
WELL I'M ACTUALLY UP FOR TALKING THIS TIME.
Gawk
Gawk
WHAAAT!?
OH SHUT UP... GIVE ME A BREAK IT'S BETTER THAN THE NIGHTMARES
I BET.
WELP, YOU'RE HERE BECAUSE OF THE CONVO I HAD EARLIER ABOUT MY CHILDHOOD.

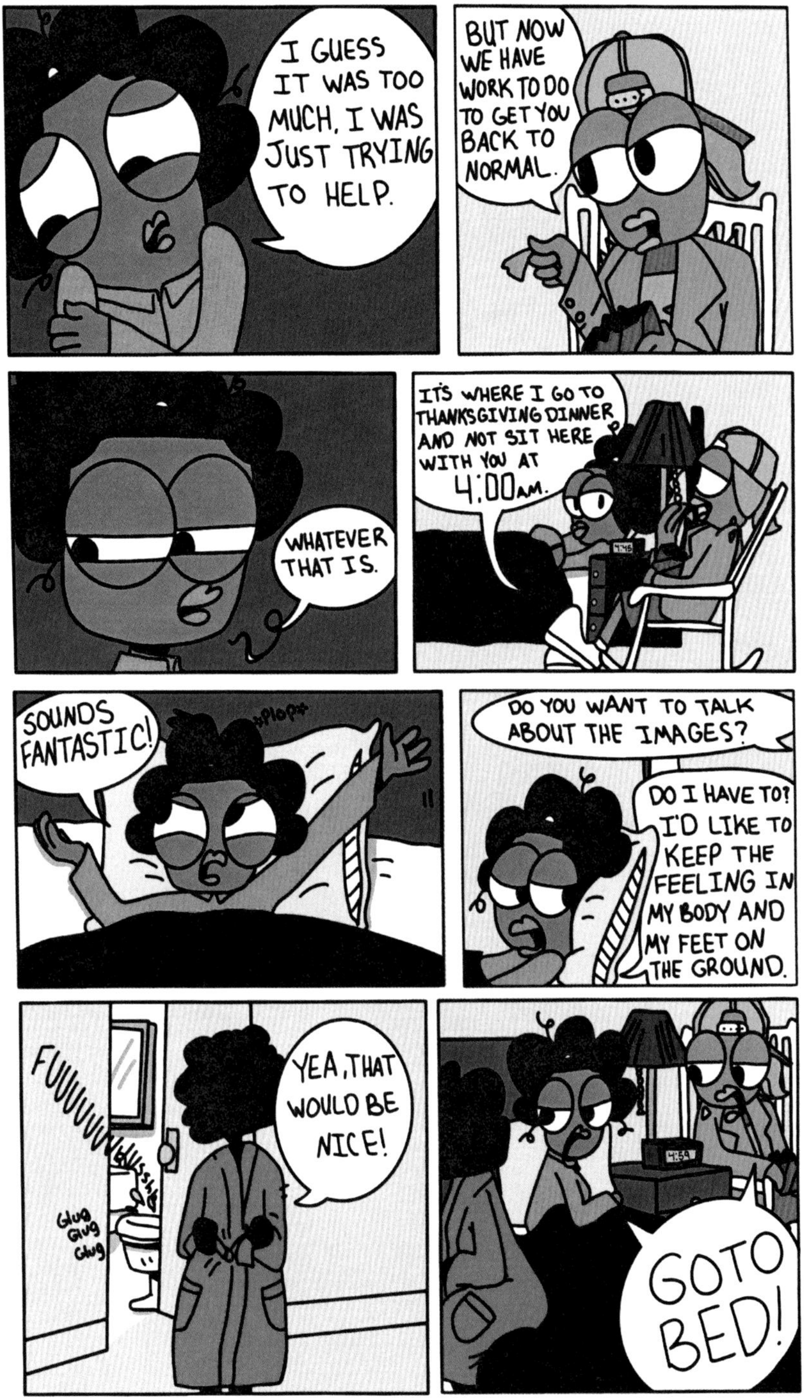
I GUESS IT WAS TOO MUCH. I WAS JUST TRYING TO HELP.
BUT NOW WE HAVE WORK TO DO TO GET YOU BACK TO NORMAL.
WHATEVER THAT IS.
IT'S WHERE I GO TO THANKSGIVING DINNER AND NOT SIT HERE WITH YOU AT 4:00AM.
SOUNDS FANTASTIC!
Plop
DO YOU WANT TO TALK ABOUT THE IMAGES?
DO I HAVE TO? I'D LIKE TO KEEP THE FEELING IN MY BODY AND MY FEET ON THE GROUND.
FUUUUUWHUSSSH
Glug Glug Glug
YEA, THAT WOULD BE NICE!
GO TO BED!

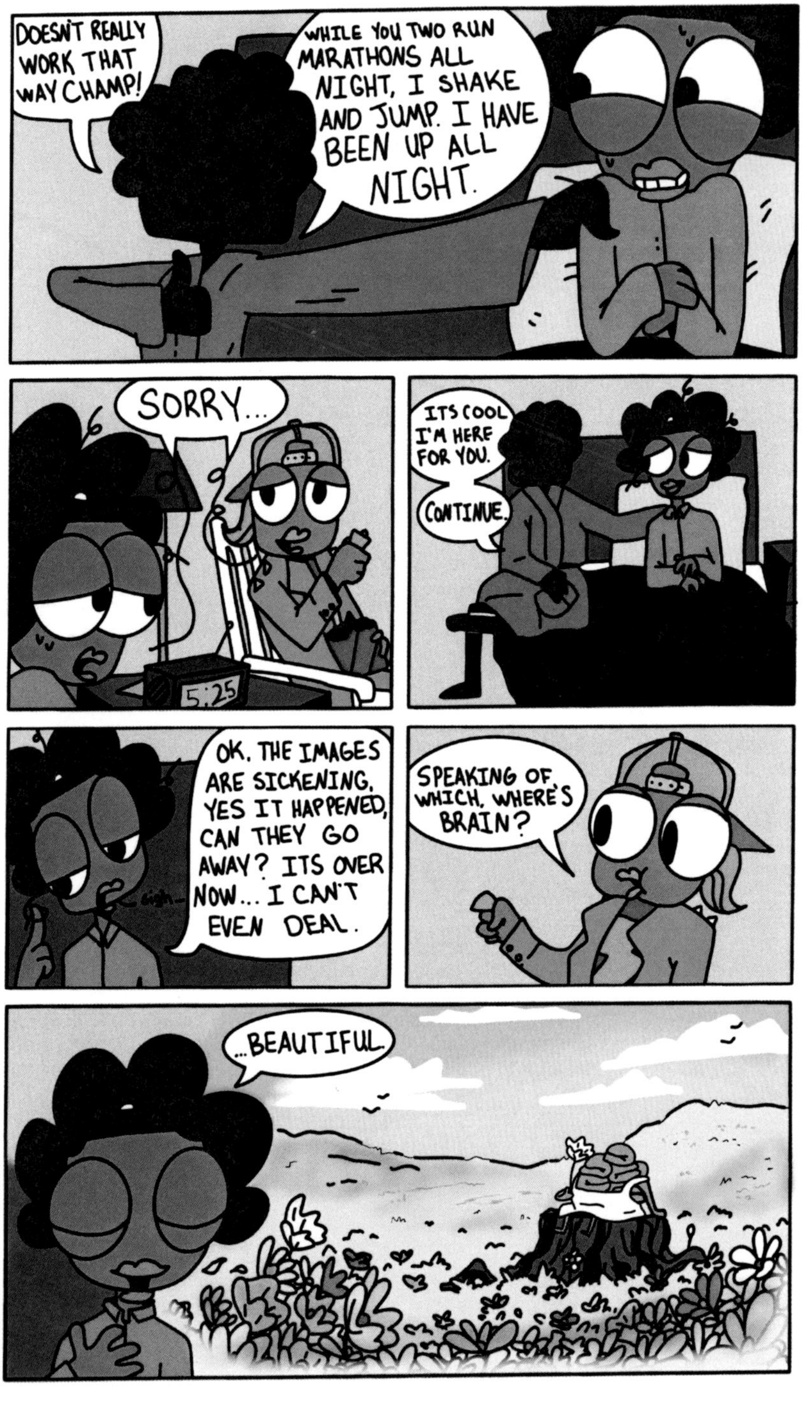
DOESN'T REALLY WORK THAT WAY CHAMP!
WHILE YOU TWO RUN MARATHONS ALL NIGHT, I SHAKE AND JUMP. I HAVE BEEN UP ALL NIGHT.
SORRY...
5:25
ITS COOL I'M HERE FOR YOU.
CONTINUE.
OK. THE IMAGES ARE SICKENING. YES IT HAPPENED, CAN THEY GO AWAY? ITS OVER NOW... I CAN'T EVEN DEAL.
sigh...
SPEAKING OF, WHICH, WHERE'S BRAIN?
...BEAUTIFUL.

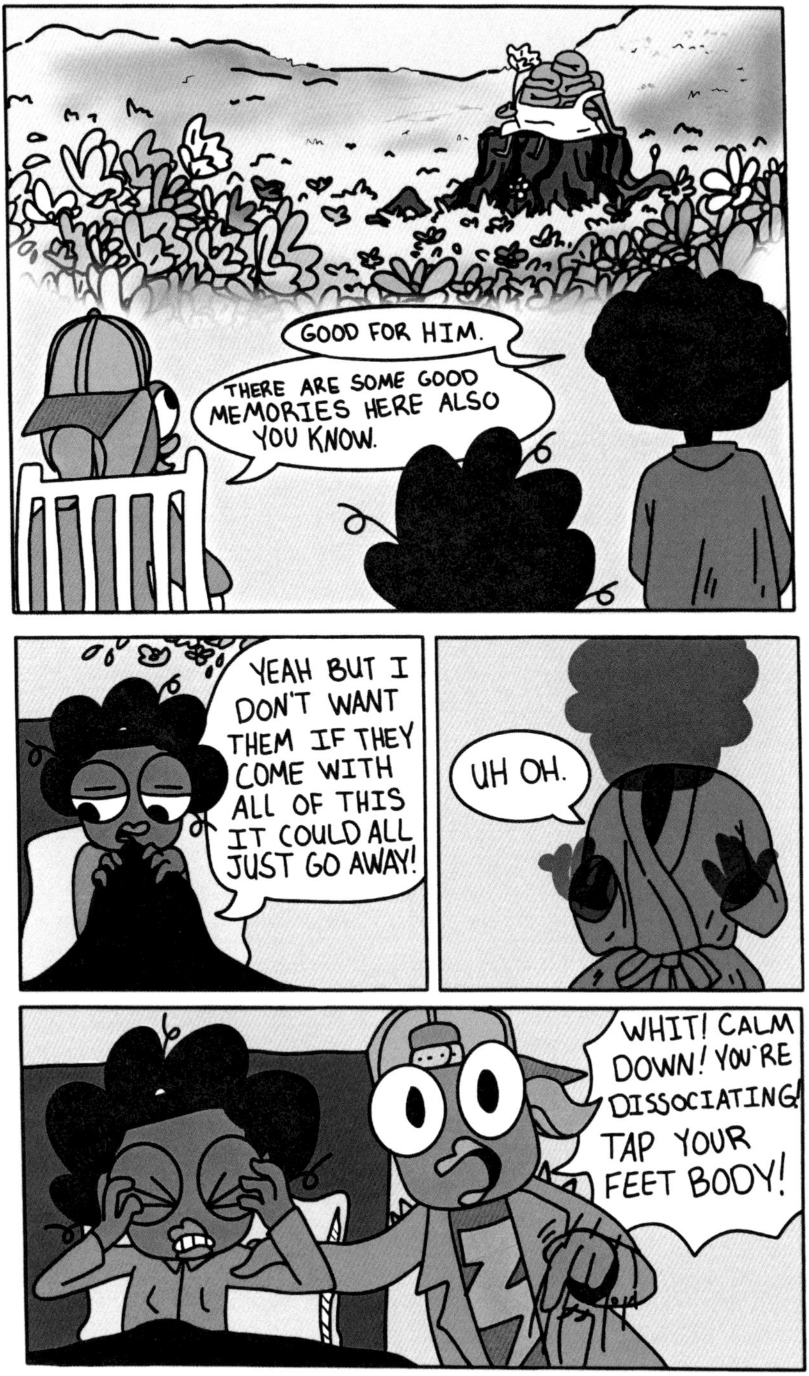
GOOD FOR HIM.
THERE ARE SOME GOOD MEMORIES HERE ALSO YOU KNOW.
YEAH BUT I DON'T WANT THEM IF THEY COME WITH ALL OF THIS IT COULD ALL JUST GO AWAY!
UH OH.
WHIT! CALM DOWN! YOU'RE DISSOCIATING! TAP YOUR FEET BODY!

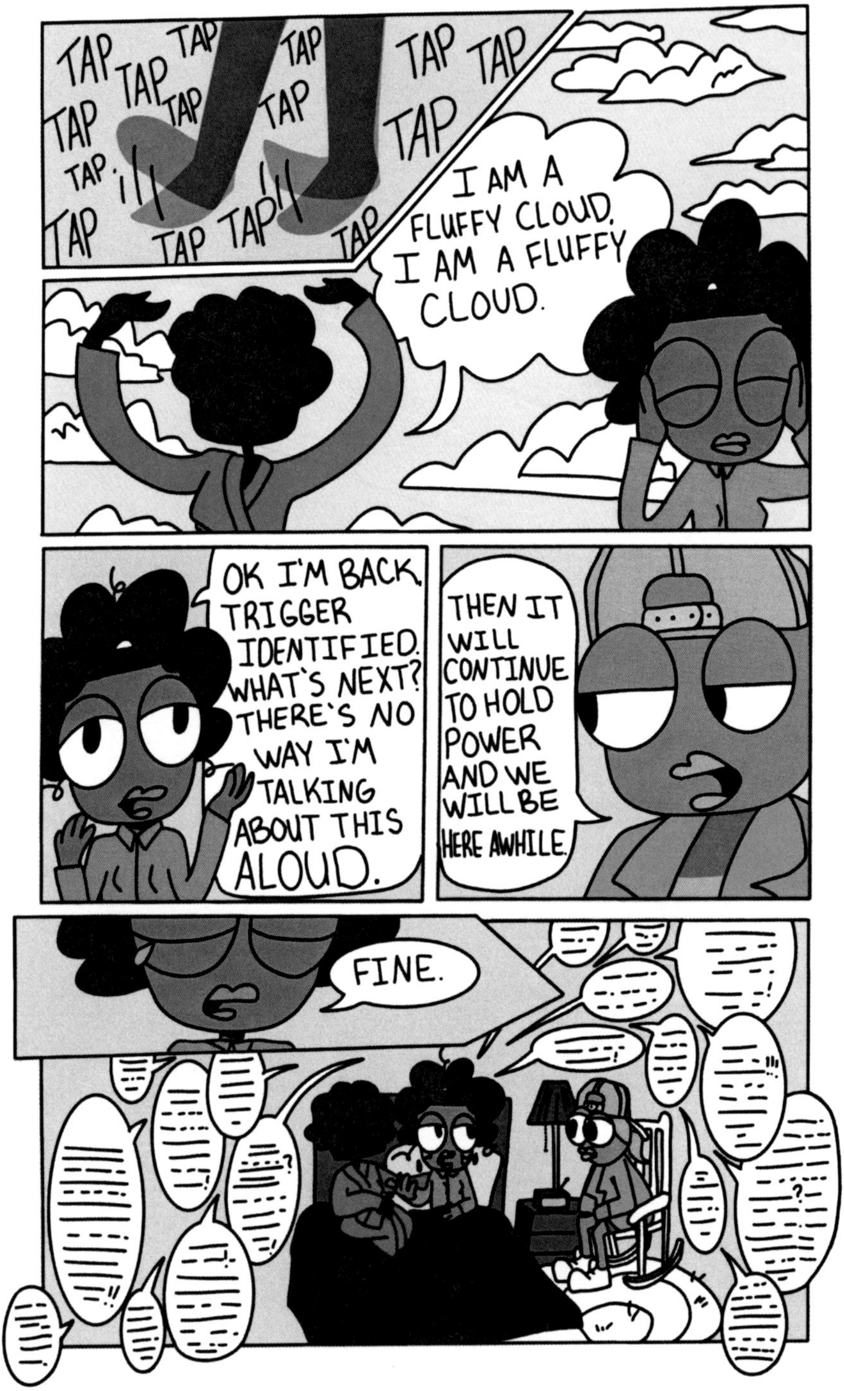
TAP TAP TAP TAP TAP TAP TAP TAP TAP TAP TAP TAP TAP TAP TAP TAP
I AM A FLUFFY CLOUD. I AM A FLUFFY CLOUD.
OK I'M BACK. TRIGGER IDENTIFIED. WHAT'S NEXT? THERE'S NO WAY I'M TALKING ABOUT THIS ALOUD.
THEN IT WILL CONTINUE TO HOLD POWER AND WE WILL BE HERE AWHILE.
FINE.

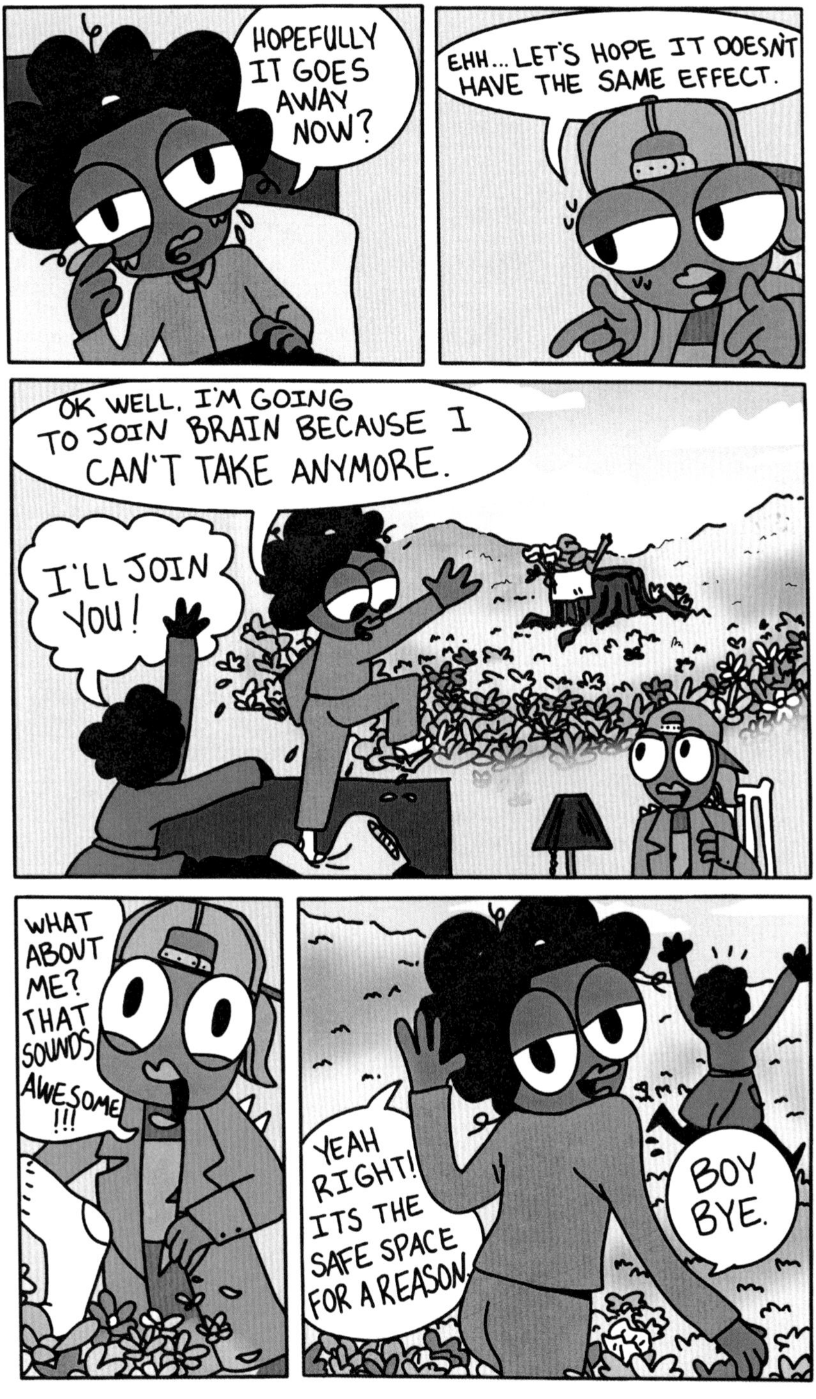
HOPEFULLY IT GOES AWAY NOW?
EHH... LET'S HOPE IT DOESN'T HAVE THE SAME EFFECT.
OK WELL. I'M GOING TO JOIN BRAIN BECAUSE I CAN'T TAKE ANYMORE.
I'LL JOIN YOU!
WHAT ABOUT ME? THAT SOUNDS AWESOME!!!
YEAH RIGHT! ITS THE SAFE SPACE FOR A REASON.
BOY BYE.

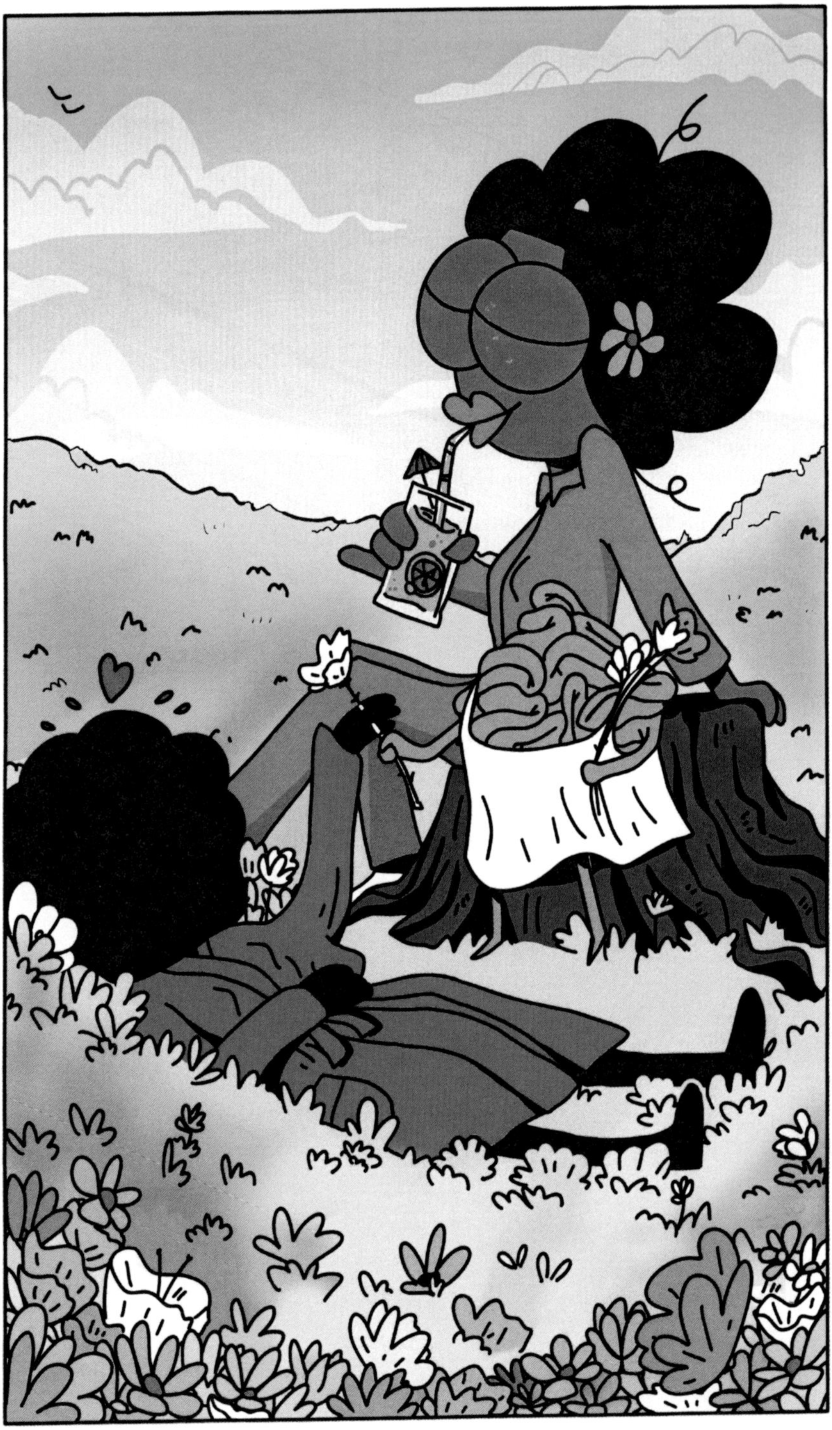

Made in United States
North Haven, CT
30 March 2022

17714997R00035